Daughter from Afar

Daughter from Afar

※

A Family's International Adoption Story

Sarah Lynn Woodard

Writers Club Press

San Jose New York Lincoln Shanghai

Daughter from Afar
A Family's International Adoption Story

Writers Club Press
an imprint of iUniverse, Inc.

For information address:
iUniverse, Inc.
5220 S. 16th St., Suite 200
Lincoln, NE 68512
www.iuniverse.com

Cover design by Brad Boutwell.

ISBN: 0-595-24543-9

Printed in the United States of America

To my daughter,
Adelynn Chen-Ge Woodard
With love and squeezes from Momma

An invisible red thread connects those who are destined to meet,
regardless of time, place or circumstance.
The thread may stretch or tangle,
but will never break.
    —Chinese Legend

Contents

Preface

Writing our personal adoption story serves many purposes. During our adoption process, family and friends seemed unable to understand what we were going through. They were supportive but unable to value the milestones as we reached them. Unless they've had direct experience with an international adoption, most people know very little about what's involved. I wrote our story as if I were talking to a friend, sharing all the highs and lows of our experience. I hope reading our story helps a friend or family member of someone adopting appreciate the gift of adoption.

My other goal is to provide helpful hints and insight for families just beginning the international adoption path. When I first began the process, I was hungry for information and direction. I read a lot of "fairy tale" adoption stories but wanted to read more "real life" experiences. Most people aren't very forthcoming admitting their weaknesses and mistakes. I hope sharing my personal feelings and thoughts helps other new parents.

Documenting our story for Adelynn's benefit is very important to me. Our journey to reach her is a fascinating story, and one that should be told. I hope when she's older she'll be proud to read her story and even prouder to know that it benefited someone else.

My motives weren't entirely selfless. Writing my fears, concerns and victories was great therapy for me. I'm not a writer by profession or even hobby. The inspiration to write my thoughts came naturally. It was a wonderful project and one I'm very proud to have undertaken.

If you're in the process of adopting, have already adopted or love someone who has adopted, I hope our personal story touches you in some small way.

Acknowledgements

It was a challenge to find the time to write our adoption story. Most of my writing was done very late at night with the rest of the household fast asleep. Sitting at my computer sipping my steaming cup of peach-flavored tea, I put my thoughts and feelings in writing. It was good therapy and more beneficial to me than I had ever imagined.

I am grateful for friends and family who encouraged me to keep writing. Thank you, Jeff, for your never-ending enthusiasm and faith in me. I'm grateful for your open mindedness to allow me to share our very personal adoption experience with the world. Jeff, your love, support and nurturing help me be the person I'm meant to be. To Adelynn, I hope when you're ready to read this book that you read it with pride. Your story is remarkable. You are a beautiful Chinese-American girl of great strength and inspiration. May you always be proud of who you are. To Mom and Dad, for being incredible, loving parents and grandparents. You have enriched Adelynn's life as deeply as she has yours. Thanks, Mom, for providing me with much-needed breaks and endless support. To Charlene Lusk, I have learned so much from you. You are a true friend, always encouraging me and there when I need a sympathetic ear. What would I do without you! To Dana Creekmore, meeting your beautiful daughter, Caroline, helped make our decision to adopt from China. Thank you for supporting us during the process and for being a genuine friend. To Heather Stanton, Mark Merrifield, Carol Manning, Charles Sroufe, Rebecca Hackworth, Dustin Parkhurst, and Eileen Neighbors for offering encouragement, advice and editing services. Thanks for catching all those typos and misspelled words! To my team of friendly Internet editors who answered my plea for a random act of kindness. These lovely people offered their comments and suggestions to make this book the best it could be: Nadine Markham-Itteilag, Lisa Grant of The Writers' Collective, Barbara Howard, Cindy Echterling, Karen Mueller Bryson, Darlene Hansen, Lorilyn Bailey, Marcia Schutte, Jo Ann Hernandez, Moya Smith, Florence Hines, B.R. Montgomery, Jo Ann Hernandez, Maureen Stephenson, Ph.D., Christine Durrenberger, Bonnie Braun, Terry Vasquez, Sally Herpst, and David Chananie. And thank you Brad Boutwell for designing the book cover and building the website. Thank you!

Sarah Lynn Woodard
www.DaughterFromAfar.com

Introduction

"Hello, this is Angela," our translator said in her soft Chinese accent. "Come to my room and meet your daughter."

I hung up the phone and looked at Jeff. "She's here!"

We hurried to Angela's room. The door was already open. I peeked in and saw three baby girls being held by their beautiful Chinese caretakers. We walked in.

"Can you tell which little girl is ours?" I quietly whispered to Jeff.

Jeff shrugged his shoulders. The referral photos of Ji Chen Ge were taken several months earlier when she was only a few months old, so it was impossible to tell. Angela spoke something in Chinese to one of the nannies, and she walked over to us holding a scared little girl.

"Ji Chen Ge?" Angela asked.

"Yes!" we said in unison.

I looked at this little girl and couldn't believe we were finally meeting our daughter. She was so beautiful and small. She had dark hair with little curls and thin, tan legs. Her eyes were sad. She wore a white t-shirt, diaper, and tattered sandals. Her shoes caught my eye. They were plastic sandals with a worn Hello Kitty emblem barely attached to the top. For a child not yet walking, they seemed to have traveled many miles.

Our Love of Travel

Reading 10,000 books is not as good as traveling 10,000 miles.

——*Confucius*

Ten years ago, in my early twenties, I would never have imagined I'd be writing a book about our international adoption experience. Visiting China was furthest from my mind. And adoption, even further. When I look back at the short bursts of decisions that have shaped my life, I'm amazed at what has transpired. We didn't come to the decision to adopt a child in the usual way. Our love for traveling started it all.

When my husband, Jeff and I first married, we were filled with ambition, dreams and goals. We loved to fantasize about traveling to exotic places, refurbishing an old home and retiring early. We compiled a long list of things we wanted to accomplish during our life together. We were undecided about children in our future but kept an open mind about it.

My job in advertising frequently held sales contests to motivate the staff. International vacations were often the reward. I thought we couldn't afford to travel internationally, so the contest seemed the only way to fulfill our dream of traveling abroad. I made more sales calls, created better presentations, and worked late hours to reach the sales goal. Each time, something kept me inches away from hitting the mark.

One particular prize was a trip to Ireland, with accommodations in an elegant castle. Our sales managers enticed us with descriptions of green, rolling hills and sing-a-longs in the Irish pubs.

"I'm gonna win this trip," I boldly told Jeff. "We're going, just you wait!"

"Oh, I don't doubt you," Jeff replied with a smile. He knew when I was determined, I was unstoppable.

I diligently worked fast and furiously to meet the sales objective for this magnificent prize. When I was notified, yet again, that I had missed the goal, I was furious.

"I'm really sorry, Sarah," my manager said, holding my sales projections. "You missed it by a hair!"

I had put a lot of energy into winning those contests and was tired of losing. I jumped in my car and drove immediately to a travel agent down the street.

"What's far away and cheap?" I asked, plunking myself down in front of the agent.

"How about Europe? Ever thought of going there?"

Ironically, there was an airfare sale to anywhere in Europe. The price seemed very affordable. We could fly from Tulsa, Oklahoma to Ireland for only $400 each. I had paid more than that to fly to the East Coast. I called my husband and asked if he was game to "hop across the pond" to Europe.

"Uh, okay," he laughed. "Whatever you want to do, go for it!"

Twenty minutes later I walked out with two round trip tickets to Ireland, and accommodations in the same castle offered in the sales contest I hadn't won. Back at my office, I flaunted my airline tickets in front of my manager. "Too bad we won't be traveling together," I said with a Cheshire cat grin. He seemed surprised, annoyed and impressed, all at the same time.

Within weeks we were off to breathtaking Ireland. We drank pints of Guinness with the locals, drove on the left side of the road in our tiny rental car, and experienced the hundred shades of green in the lush rolling hills. This trip to Ireland ignited a travel obsession. I had my first taste of travel, and it merely whetted my appetite.

Finding budget travel packages for exciting destinations became a hobby of mine. I stalked the Internet for travel bargains. I opened a monthly vacation fund. We had money directly deposited from our paychecks so we wouldn't notice the loss. I became a frequent flyer expert managing half a dozen accounts, all organized by file folders. We obtained frequent flyer credit cards so each purchase would accrue miles. We charged everything we could on them and always paid them off at the end of the month.

"Is there anything you need to buy at work that you can charge on our credit card and expense?" I asked Jeff, looking for another resource of frequent flyer miles.

Jeff snapped his fingers in the realization of a good idea. "Laptops! I need ten laptops for my service guys. I can charge it on our card, we get the miles, and I can expense it at work. Everybody wins!"

"Yes!" I cheered, and did a little happy dance. Ten laptops would accrue over 10,000 miles!

The ability to fly internationally for free made our traveling very affordable. By being diligent, and a little obsessive, I found incredible deals to some fascinating places. Like Russia. The Russia package was too good to pass up. We booked it, and left two weeks later.

While in Russia, we made friends with two gentlemen visiting from New York. They were in their early fifties and were in Russia taking advantage of the same great travel deal we found. We teamed up with them and toured the country together. The four of us bundled up in multiple layers, and walked the beautiful streets of St. Petersburg.

Jeff and I, and our two friends, Charles and Nat, bunked in an overnight train to Moscow. The compartment was tiny, with bunk beds on each side. We giggled as we all crammed into our new sleeping quarters.

"I get a top bunk," I requested, seeing a heating vent located at the top. We settled into our beds, and pulled the scratchy wool blankets over ourselves to keep warm. We laughed and told stories until the swaying of the train lulled us to sleep.

Once in Moscow, the four of us toured Red Square and Saint Basil's Cathedral.

We stood in front of the famous cathedral and stared.

"Unbelievable," Jeff muttered under his breath. "I can't believe we're really here."

"This is one of those life changing events, isn't it?" I whispered to Jeff.

"Yup," he said, as he grabbed my hand buried within my giant, insulated glove.

At the end of our journey, we sadly said goodbye to our new friends. We felt inspired by them. They were full of life and adventure, having traveled all over the world. They thought nothing of landing in a foreign country by themselves and traveling wherever they felt inclined with nothing but a backpack and a dream.

"Life is not a dress rehearsal," Charles would say. And he was right.

Their zest for the unknown was contagious. We kept in touch by email, as we made plans for future adventures. We eventually traveled with Charles and Nat to Africa and Iran. We rode through Africa on safari, catching a glimpse of sleeping leopards hanging from the trees and having morning tea at sunrise on the Masai Mara. We crossed the desert of Iran, with me dressed in the mandatory chador, completely covered in black flowing fabric from head to toe. While sitting on beautifully woven carpets, we smoked pipes with apple-flavored tobacco and chatted with the warm, loving Persians.

Our chance meeting with these two friends changed our lives indefinitely. They motivated us to explore every corner of the world. We became better people by experiencing other cultures and meeting individuals we never would have come in contact with otherwise. Traveling was truly a life-long gift. In five short years Jeff and I explored all seven continents.

Visiting China

If there is righteousness in the soul,
there will be beauty in the character.
If there is beauty in the character,
there will be harmony in the house.
If there is harmony in the house,
there will be order in the nation.
If there is order in the nation,
there will be peace in the world.

——*Confucius*

Our first thoughts of adopting a daughter from China came during a visit to the People's Republic of China in the spring of 1998. This was our third international trip. Doing my usual travel bargain search, a certain package caught my eye. I found a vacation package for two that included round trip airfare to Beijing with a week of hotel, food and touring for less than $1,600! I had never thought of traveling to China, but visiting the Great Wall sounded exhilarating. My husband wasn't as excited about China.

"China?" Jeff asked with disbelief. "Didn't their government open fire on a bunch of students in Tiananmen Square a few years ago?"

I couldn't help but sigh. "I'm ready for an adventure," I insisted. "I feel like something is pulling us there."

Neither of us knew anything about traveling to China. After weeks of giving Jeff my sales pitch, he finally relented.

"Okay, I'll go," he said flatly. "But if we die, it's your fault!" He shook a scolding finger at me and smiled. We both laughed. I gave him a big hug and told him I'd take full responsibility. He had learned that my crazy ideas almost always turned out to be exciting and fun.

When we told our families about our plans to visit China, they immediately worried. Jeff and I come from a long line of worriers. Only months after a visit to Australia, this would be our first trip to a non-English speaking country. They thought we were crazy and attempted to talk us out of the trip. I hated to cause them sleepless nights but I felt we were destined to go.

We arrived in Beijing and were stunned. It felt like stepping into a dream. Street signs, billboards, and storefronts, all written in Chinese. No English. We were clueless. Thousands of people pedaled by on their bicycles, and not one bike looked less than twenty years old. They all appeared brown, rusty and worn. Some people had backpacks thrown over their shoulders, while others were carrying passengers who stood on little pegs protruding from the back wheels. The bicycles were their most effective means of transportation. We noticed many bikes had tiny flatbeds on the back, used for hauling. One man, looking to be in his sixties, carried a refrigerator on the back of his bike. His skinny, hairless legs rhythmically pedaled, as the bike squeaked and wobbled.

In addition to all the bicyclers, many people milled about on foot. Many people squatted instead of sitting as if it were preferred and more comfortable. It was lunchtime, and many squatted, eating rice with their chopsticks.

"How do their legs stand that?" Jeff asked, amazed that this position was comfortable to them.

"It must be something genetic or developed with years of practice," I guessed.

I had just visited the toilets, so knew first hand the unnatural "squat." In the bathroom, there were no toilets, only an open trough to squat over. I had difficulty maintaining dignity in this position, and the women weren't shy about watching.

I now understood the meaning of "culture shock." We were totally out of our element. We walked among a sea of black heads, most significantly shorter than us. I felt very conspicuous. A small crowd of people gathered around us pointing at my red hair, "a beacon beckoning a closer look." Wherever we walked, school children, who had obviously been studying English in school, giggled and ran about us, speaking English in their strange-sounding accents. We could make out many of the words and phrases they happily used to impress us.

The children were quite delightful, but the adults just stared. The stares were not unfriendly, because they all smiled and bowed, but they stared in a way that seemed to say, "Aren't you funny-looking people?" I'd give them my warmest smile, and it was always returned.

China has a beautiful culture, rich in history. Visiting the Great Wall of China was humbling. The wall is a piece of history built over 2,000 years ago in the seventh century B.C. It's one of the Seven Wonders of the World, stretching over 1,500 miles, up and down mountains, at incredibly steep angles. We walked along the wall, and chose to climb to a higher area with a spectacular view. The climb up was so difficult, we stopped several times to catch our breath. When we finally reached the top, we could only stare.

"Oh, my!" I whispered with such awe my voice broke. "This is the most spectacular view I've ever seen in my life." Tears filled my eyes, and Jeff wasn't exactly dry-eyed when he glanced at me.

"Wow!" he said, his voice low, "Look at that! The wall stretches across the mountains as far as the eye can see. This can be seen from outer space! No picture can do this justice."

I took a deep breath and replied, "Jeff, we're actually standing on the Great Wall of China! Aren't you glad now that we came to China?" He nodded, as overcome by the awesome panorama as I.

We spent some time soaking up the experience and then began the trek down. I worried I wouldn't make it, but I had no choice. Facing steps that looked too steep to safely walk down, Jeff took my arm.

"Sit," he instructed, "and scoot down a step at a time, the way a child goes down stairs. You aren't very graceful even on a good day!"

I didn't argue, and scooted down alongside my husband. He held onto my arm, so I wouldn't lose my balance. Even so, my legs felt like putty, shaking and trembling from the physical strain. As we descended the wall, we looked up at the elevated portion we had just climbed.

"We made it," I said panting. "I feel quite impressed with myself. My scrawny little legs made it up and back down again. Unbelievable!" We held hands and walked to catch our bus. The experience was exhilarating!

We enjoyed wandering around the cities of China. I loved to sit and watch the people going on about their day. Little family-owned shops along the sidewalk are no larger than walk-in closets, but brimming with wares. Their merchandise is stuffed into a small concrete building, looking more like a flea market than an actual store. Old people hang their bird-cages in the trees of the small community parks. The trees are filled with singing caged birds experiencing a taste of freedom. For babies not yet potty trained, the world is their toilet. Instead of diapers, their pants are split open at the crotch. The toddlers squat and go whenever they feel the urge. I loved to see their little bare cheeks peeking out of their pants but was careful where I stepped.

We passed two young girls, maybe ten years old, squatting while eating their lunches. They eagerly waved, and we waved back. I noticed they seemed to be nibbling on some type of meat. The meat looked like a chicken's foot. My eyes widened in shock, and I pointed to their lunch.

"Chicken feet?" I asked in disbelief.

They looked at each other and giggled but didn't seem to understand me. I made flapping movements with my arms and strutted around like a chicken.

"Chicken?" I asked again.

"Yes, yes," they replied, full of laughs and smiles as they continued to gnaw on the toe of the chicken.

"Yuck!" I laughed, with my eyes wide in disgust.

The children covered their mouths with their hands and shook with laughter. They thought it hilarious that they had caused me to grimace and hold my stomach to still its queasy stirring. One of the girls pretended to make the chicken foot dance, and the other thought that was a great show and did the same. We all laughed together.

"Nothing like dancing dead chicken feet to break a language barrier," I chuckled to Jeff as we waved goodbye and walked away.

Jeff and I made it a point to wake up early in the morning to watch people doing Tai Chi exercises in the park. It's a graceful sight as their bodies slowly glide with controlled strength. The peacefulness of the exercises is in stark contrast to the sounds and sights of the congested, polluted city.

The bulging population made me feel claustrophobic. Personal space is a luxury the Chinese cannot afford. Riding on the city bus became impossible for me. The bus was packed full of people, pressed against us on every side. I gripped a sticky black handle and held on as the bus jerked and teetered. The trapped feeling made me break out in a sweat and induced a migraine.

In America, we generally keep two to three feet from each other out of respect for personal space. While riding in an elevator with a stranger in the U.S., we stand on opposite sides and give each other some room. In China, however, it is so crowded that someone is pushed up against you at all times. While riding on the elevator in our hotel a Chinese man stepped in. We exchanged nods, and he stood so close that the top of his head was right below my chin. I could see tiny white flakes of dandruff resting in the part of his black hair. I shifted the weight on my feet and nonchalantly stepped back away from him. It was a challenge not to get anxious about someone being "in my space." It's an entirely different way of life.

The drastically overpopulated country has limited clean water, housing, work and living space for its population. Basic needs are in short supply. Although the locals have adapted to the situation, the water is not safe to drink. For showering, we were cautioned to keep our mouths closed to prevent ingesting parasites that could come from accidentally swallowing water. We also brushed our teeth with bottled water.

"Don't drink the buggies," I jokingly reminded Jeff, as I tied a sock around the faucet to remind us not to drink from it.

Most people in the cities live in tall white, cinderblock apartment buildings, which are stained from the city's pollutants. The water and sewer systems are less than ideal. It is not unusual for a family of eight to live in a studio-sized apartment. The apartment buildings are littered with clothes hanging to dry outside the windows. As someone who uses laundry detergent, scented bleach, fabric softener, and fragrant dryer sheets, I cringed seeing the clothes dangling in the automobile exhaust. The pollution is choking. It wasn't uncommon to see people wearing facemasks to protect themselves from the heavy smog and exhaust.

I had heard about China's "one-child policy" before we visited the country, but never gave it much thought. Often, when we hear about hardships so far removed from our own lives, we dismiss them. While in China, I could see and understand firsthand the need for a one-child-per-family policy.

China's population problem began many years ago. A large family was once considered a sign of prosperity and happiness. In the 1960's, during the Cultural Revolution, the country's leader, Chairman Mao Tse-Tung encouraged the people to have many children to "make China strong." The result was massive overcrowding with limited food, water, housing and jobs to sustain the people.

In 1979, the government instituted a one-child-per-family policy to limit the population growth and to ensure that China would be able to feed its people. It seemed like a drastic step, but something had to be done. The policy's slogan "one is best, don't exceed two" encourages one-child per family, later marriages, and spacing between births. People in special circumstances, ethnic minorities and rural families are often allowed more than one child.

In order to enforce this one-child policy, women are required to obtain a permit to have a child and then must bring the "birth permission paper" to the hospital at the time of her delivery.[1] A family with an unauthorized pregnancy could face terrible consequences. If discovered, forced late term abortion, sterilization, increased taxes, or loss of employment could result. The family will be forced to pay a fine for that child, costing as much as eight times the annual salary for the average worker. The Chinese government provides for the healthcare and schooling of the first authorized child, but a second child is not entitled to these benefits. Families wanting more than one child need to pay for the second child's schooling and healthcare. Many unauthorized second children are being hidden from the system. The family may squeeze out enough money to pay for their children's education for a few years, but it's very difficult. Considering the fee, healthcare and schooling, only the wealthy are able to afford a second child.

Chinese families have traditionally preferred male children to female children. Some of the reasons for this preference include the carrying on of the family name, the boy's ability to handle a heavier workload in the rural communities, ancestral worship, and inheritance laws that pass property to males, and rarely to females.

In Chinese culture, the son is customarily responsible for the care of his parents in their old age. This is critical since China does little to provide assistance for the elderly, and most people do not have enough money to support themselves when they're older. Many generations may live under one roof, with the older family members helping with household chores and caring for children. Dynamics are changing, and nursing homes are becoming more common in China, but living with the extended family is still preferred. The older members thrive in this environment where they are able to contribute and be useful. But if the family has just a daughter, there may be no one to care for them in their old age as the daughter is expected to care for her husband's parents instead. Many Chinese are perfectly happy if their first-born child is a girl. It's important to remember the preference for a boy is a traditional attitude going back to the time of Confucius. Just as in the U.S., some people hold different values than others.

Those in favor of the one-child policy point to statistics that illustrate the policy has effectively reduced China's population by 250 million. This has alleviated some of the stress on China, which already comprises one-fifth of the world's population. Those who criticize the policy claim it has led to extensive human rights violations and sexual discrimination. The number of abandoned baby girls is astonishing.

Prenatal scanning to determine the sex of the baby is illegal in China but performed nonetheless. Ultrasound machines are readily available to identify the sex of the fetus in the womb.[2] Determining the sex by ultrasound is commonly possible in the fourth, fifth or sixth month of pregnancy, often resulting in late-term abortions.[3] This practice is causing a sex imbalance in China, as more boys are born than girls. According to China's 2000 census, 117 Chinese boys were born for every 100 Chinese girls.[4] In the rural areas where kinship and ancestral worship remain strong, the imbalance is as high as 144 boys born for every 100 girls. These figures are way above the worldwide average.

If a mother gives birth to an unauthorized or unwanted baby girl, she may choose to illegally abandon the child. This might be because the baby exceeded the one-child policy. Or, the mother may abandon the firstborn in hopes of trying again for a son. Parents who do not want a baby girl may leave the child in a public place where she will be quickly found. Many babies are found in highly populated areas like busy streets, markets, bus stations or in front of public buildings. The family may abandon the child hoping she will find another home, as this is their only way of making an adoption plan for the child. If the birth mother is caught she could face terrible consequences. The mothers take huge risks to offer their babies a chance at a future and to make sure they will survive. They care enough to save them but can't risk the consequences of keeping them. Most abandonments occur within the first two months of life, usually within the first few days. Typically, the baby is found and taken to the nearest orphanage. In addition to girls, a number of handicapped, deformed, unhealthy babies and some boys are abandoned as well.

The Chinese government estimates that over 20,000 children are living in orphanages. Experts believe the actual number to be over five times that figure.[5] The conditions of the orphanages in China vary greatly. Many of the orphanages in larger cities with greater financial support provide nutritious food and proper medical care. In ideal circumstances, the children have loving caretakers who become very attached to the children. Non-profit organizations around the world aid some of China's orphanages by providing education, staff, food and medical supplies. Children in these orphanages are being well loved and cared for, considering their circumstances. However, in areas of extreme poverty, the level of care is greatly reduced. The institutions located in the poor, rural communities can have unspeakable conditions. They may not have medicines to treat something as simple as an ear infection, so many of the children are sick. Additionally, the children may be fed only what is available and affordable at the local market. Rice congee, which is rice boiled down into a watery paste, is often a staple of orphanage food. The boiling leaves little nutrients or flavor. Many children are weak and malnourished. The physical care of the babies in these orphanages is minimal, and the emotional care is even less. Orphanages are often understaffed and under funded so the child's own will to survive is essential.

In 1985 the Chinese government made it possible for these orphans to be adopted internationally. Since then, foreigners have adopted over 30,000 Chinese orphans, most of them coming to America. In 2000, U.S.

parents adopted over 5,000 babies. China is currently the leading country in international adoptions.[6]

The one-child policy seems harsh, yet essential for the viability of the country. Our trip to China was intended to be another eye opening cultural experience and it was. We were learning the harsh realities faced by the Chinese people. To think about the children in the orphanages saddened me. The idea of adopting crept into my mind.

"Why couldn't we adopt a child instead of giving birth to one?" I secretly pondered. It didn't seem right to bring more children into the world when there were tens of thousands needing homes. I kept my thoughts to myself and didn't mention them to Jeff. I needed more time to think about this.

On our last day in China, we visited a kindergarten class. It was part of a tour showing visitors China's school system. When we walked in, the children went wild. They were thrilled to see us, bouncing up and down, waving their arms, yelling, "Hello! Hello!" We were overwhelmed by the greeting.

"Hello," I said back warmly. Two little girls ran to my side and grabbed my hands. One of the girls looked at me with wide eyes as she stroked my long fingers. She placed her hand up against mine, as if to measure the size. Her tiny hand was smaller than my palm. She was amazed and frightened at the difference.

"BIG," I dramatically said. She seemed to understand and nodded with an open mouthed stare. I then lifted my foot high in the air.

"BIGGER," I exclaimed as I pointed to my large foot.

"Oooooo," she squealed and ran to gather the other children. They came running and surrounded me. I lifted my size twelve foot in the air and the shrieks of laughter filled the room. The children held their feet up against mine and roared with belly laughs. Compared to them, I truly looked like a giant. I'm not sure who laughed harder, but it was a wonderful experience. The teacher shouted instructions in Chinese, and the children scurried around taking their places. They sat in a circle on the floor and sang Chinese songs. They smiled, clapped and made the appropriate movements to the song. It was delightful! As I watched the children, I felt a little tug at my heart.

I was both grateful and somber leaving China. It would be wonderful to be home with clean water, fresh air, good food, and wide-open spaces. But I would miss the kind people of China. I savored experiencing this unique culture.

On the flight home, I noticed an American family seated in front of us with a small Asian girl. I admit, I was eavesdropping and listened to them tell their story to a passenger across the aisle. They were traveling home with their newly adopted daughter from China. As I listened, the little girl played peek-a-boo with me over the seat. She appeared to be less than two years old. She was beautiful, with chubby cheeks, sleek black hair, and a sweetness in her eyes I can't describe.

"Boo!" I said as her head poked between the seats. She laughed and darted back out of sight. Adopting from China entered my mind, again.

"What do you think about having a little cutie like that in our house?" I whispered to Jeff. He looked at me in shock.

"A baby?" he asked in disbelief. "Ah, oh, are we having the kid discussion?"

"Oh, I don't know," I shrugged. "It's just been on my mind."

Jeff looked blankly at me. He enjoyed living life as a DINK (Dual Income No Kids). He wasn't ready to be a parent yet. Neither was I, but I could feel myself warming up to the idea, and the idea of adopting felt right.

When we returned from China, the abandonments caused by the "one-child policy" haunted me. I felt a strong pull to China, and I couldn't stop thinking about the many babies waiting for the loving arms of parents. I read on the Internet about the effects of the policy and how the children were suffering. This passage from an article written by Laura Beck, Nancy D'Antonio, and Lynne Lyon is heart wrenching.

Imagine that you are but a few days old, and you wake up alone on the sidewalk or in a bus station. Instead of the familiar smell, heartbeat and arms of your mother to comfort you when you cry, no one comes for what seems like an eternity. When someone finally notices you, it is a stranger. Imagine then, that for the next 6 or more months you are confined to a crib where you are cared for sporadically by many people who also care for many other babies. No one picks you up when you cry. You are not fed when you are hungry, but fed when it is convenient for your caregiver. You are not held enough or loved enough. And when you are scared at night because of the dark and the crying of other babies, you are left to comfort yourself.[7]

I couldn't push the image from my mind. I had to go back to China.

◆   ◆   ◆

We scheduled another trip to China a year later to visit the southern part of the country. We flew on a Chinese airline to Guangzhou, China. The airline was fine, but the seating was built for a smaller sized individual. Jeff and I are each close to six feet tall. Sitting up straight, my knees hit the back of the seat in front of me. The confinement gave me motion sickness.

The majority of the passengers were Chinese, primarily men. In China, hacking and spitting in the streets is common. The men on the plane apparently felt the floor of the airplane would work just as well. I'm open to experiencing cultural differences, but this was too much. During our flight, the hacking, coughing and spitting intensified my motion sickness.

"Is this going to go on the entire 15 hours?" I asked Jeff, as I sipped ginger ale to settle my stomach.

"I don't see how they could have anything left. They've been hacking for hours," Jeff mumbled as he turned his head to avoid witnessing another blob hit the floor. The 15-hour flight was grueling.

Once safely on the ground and out of spitting distance, we traveled by boat along the Yangtze River. We watched the building of the Three Gorges Dam and stopped to visit the small riverside villages. Poverty in these struggling communities is numbing. It was life and death poverty right before our eyes. We passed a community meat market where pieces of raw chicken were stacked on tables in the open air. There was absolutely no refrigeration, and flies swarmed around the rancid smelling meat. Fish floated in buckets of water, still alive, but beginning to curl and float on their sides. The smell of the stagnant water in the buckets was as pungent as the rotted fish. We passed a table full of gutted frogs and roasted rats on a stick.

"Oh, God," I gasped, "I think I'm going to hurl!"

I felt the blood drain from my face and thought I might faint. I covered my nose. Jeff has often teased me about my keen sense of smell. I can sniff out the ingredients of any recipe or pinpoint someone with bad breath in a crowded room. This was not the place to have a sensitive nose! Jeff handed me a box of Altoid mints.

"Try these," he suggested. "They say they're curiously strong mints. Let's see just how strong they are!"

The mints helped to cover up the smell a little and settled my stomach. Jeff spotted a skinned cat outstretched on a cart.

"Okay, we're outta here," he shouted and grabbed my arm.

"What?" I asked in confusion. "What is it?"

Jeff shoved me through the crowd to prevent me from seeing the cat. I'm not a cat lover, but seeing that would have pushed me over the edge. The Chinese are very resourceful to find all sources of protein and nourishment. The luxury of pets that we have in the U.S. is not shared with those in many other parts of the world.

The pollution in the riverside towns is appalling. The Chinese burn coal as their source of fuel to heat and cook. People are seen hauling heavy loads of it on the back of bicycles. Small, round discs of black coal are stacked up outside homes. As the coal burns, black smoke is released into the air, leaving a haze over the city. As we walked along the neighborhood streets, my lungs tightened as if I were having an asthmatic attack. Jeff and I both became ill with upper respiratory infections from the extreme pollution. Within days my throat burned from breathing the air and my voice became raspy. We definitely take for granted the clean air we enjoy and the laws put in place to protect our environment in the United States. In these poorer countries, trying to cook a meal to feed a family has greater immediate priority than being ecologically friendly.

Despite our health challenges, we enjoyed the people and culture of southern China. We found them to be kind and generous despite the obvious financial disparity between our two cultures. They enjoyed practicing their English and we welcomed the interaction. They were as fascinated by us as we were by them. The experience of a different way of life was enriching. Watching people work in less than ideal conditions, breathing the choking air, and examining the exotic foods made me aware of what luxuries we take for granted on a daily basis. I was impressed with what little they had materially, but how happy they were without it. My pouting over not having a pair of matching shoes to go with my outfit seemed trivial and shallow. This was a well-needed wake-up call. There is something to be said for the beauty of simplicity. We watched a willowy Chinese man push his tiny boat down the river with a large stick, a single hanging lantern illuminating his work as he fished for the day's meal. His worn and leathery hand rose to say "Ni Hao," or hello. I waved back and goose bumps ran up my arms.

On the flight home, I again thought about China's extreme poverty and its one-child policy. There were many girls in orphanages waiting for families and I was feeling ready to become a parent. Was Jeff? I had a successful career but had long since been disenchanted with it. I was ready for something more meaningful and substantial. Becoming a parent would be the ultimate challenge. Adopting a baby girl from China would be different from having a birth child. Jeff and I had a strong, committed marriage and I felt comfortable we could handle the uncertainty and complexities associated with an international adoption. We were drawn to China for a reason.

"What do you think about adopting a baby from China?" I blurted out while we were eating our airline food.

"A baby from China?" Jeff asked, not seeming very surprised by my question.

"Yeah, what do you think about that?" I asked again, trying to appear very matter-of-fact about my question.

"I've thought about that, too," he answered without missing a bite. "I think it sounds like something we should do."

"Me, too," I nodded, relieved at his response. Our decision was that easy! We would travel to China yet again. And the next time I'd be flying home from China, it would be with a little girl in my arms.

Our Decision

○ ○

Be not afraid of growing slowly, be afraid only of standing still.

—*Chinese proverb*

Upon returning from our second trip to China, I researched the adopting process.

"Are you sure you're okay with adopting a baby girl from China instead of conceiving our own child?" I questioned Jeff.

"Yeah," Jeff shrugged his reply, "I don't have a need to replicate my genes. A child is a child. That's all that matters."

I was pleased his response mirrored my feelings. Jeff and I had long discussions. We felt adopting an abandoned baby girl from China was the path we were supposed to take. We had never tried to conceive a child. Adoption was our first choice. After traveling to so many countries and seeing how many children around the world need homes, it seemed only right for us to provide a home to a child who needed one. Once again we were drawn to China.

I researched adoption agencies on the Internet. It was important to choose an agency that had experience in Chinese adoptions and in providing emotional support through the process. I knew two families who had adopted from a local international adoption agency. Dillon International[8] was one of the best in the country, and we were fortunate to have them located in our own community. A non-profit agency, they provide extensive support to families once the children are home. I checked their website and studied the process for adopting from China. I requested an information packet and read it from cover to cover. Then I filed it away. We planned to adopt, but we weren't able to take the next step. A child was a big commitment. We enjoyed traveling around the world, plodding around in our flower garden, and spending leisurely evenings together. We didn't feel ready just yet.

Four months after our vacation in China, Jeff was called out of town unexpectedly for work on the Fourth of July weekend. Jeff was scheduled to return home on Monday. I went to the airport to pick him up but discovered his flight had been delayed for more than an hour. I decided to walk around the terminal and kill time until his plane landed. Walking around, I noticed a group of people gathering at one of the gates holding balloons and cameras. I always love watching homecomings when people are reunited with friends and families. I stopped to watch. To my surprise, a couple holding the most beautiful little girl I had ever seen stepped off the plane to a crowd of cheers. My eyes instantly filled with tears. I knew this was the homecoming of a newly adopted Chinese girl. I stood close by and listened to every word the mother said.

"She loves Neal," I heard the mother say as she pointed to a teenage boy who was obviously her older son. "She's two years old and can't roll over in bed, walk or even crawl," she explained somberly.

The new parents described their journey through China to their family and friends. The crowd was touched and excited to have this new addition home. Someone handed the little girl a shiny balloon, and she tugged at it in amazement. As the group and family headed toward the baggage area, I nonchalantly walked with them. I followed, pretending to be looking for my own luggage. I just couldn't take my eyes off that little girl and was overwhelmed with emotion at witnessing this happy homecoming. The family gathered their heavy, well-traveled luggage into a waiting car and hoisted their new little girl into a car seat.

When they finally left, I went back to Jeff's gate to wait for his plane. When he stepped off the plane, I was brimming with excitement to tell him all about what he had just missed. We walked hand in hand down the terminal as I described my feelings about the homecoming. Jeff was tired from his trip, but shared in my enthusiasm.

After witnessing the homecoming I knew it was time for us to take the next step. I asked Jeff if he'd be willing to attend one of the Dillon International pre-adoption workshops.

"I think we should adopt from China when we decide to have children," he objected, "but I'm enjoying our life the way it is." Adding a child to our life would certainly change things.

"Let's just go and see what happens," I suggested, hoping the workshop would motivate us to take the next step. The pre-adoption workshop would be a great general overview about adopting internationally. We decided to attend the October session.

I was nervous and oddly embarrassed attending the workshop. We walked in and sat in the front row. There were about a dozen couples and a few single ladies seated for the presentation. The Dillon International staff conducting the pre-adoption workshop understood what a big step this was for many families attending. Families choose adoption for different reasons, and the speakers were sensitive to this.

The first half of the workshop program was a seminar type format. The social workers explained in general terms the process for adopting internationally. Dillon International provides assistance with adopting from various countries besides China, so they highlighted each country they represent. I paid particularly close attention to information about their China program.

After the intermission, about a dozen families entered the room. These were families who had adopted children from many countries, such as Ukraine, Guatemala, India, Korea and China. They came to share their personal experiences and help answer questions. The family representing China was ironically the family I saw come home that night in July! I was startled to see them at the seminar.

"That's the family," I nudged Jeff, "the family I saw come home last July!" I couldn't believe my eyes!

The little girl was still the cutest thing I had ever seen, and I could tell Jeff was enamored with her, too. The little girl, Caroline, was adopted from a very poor part of China. The orphanage conditions were less than ideal. When her family received her at two years old, she couldn't walk or even crawl. At the conference, just three months later, she toddled around the room like she owned the place. She wore black and orange striped leggings. The front of her dress was adorned with a bright orange, smiling pumpkin face, in celebration of Halloween. Her soft black hair held an elegant bow. She ran up to Jeff and gave him a heart-melting smile. Her mother, Dana, scooped Caroline up and brought her back to their seats, but Caroline continued to run back to Jeff. Finally, Jeff picked her up and playfully tossed her in the air. She squealed with delight, fists clenched and laughed so sweetly the conference ground to a stop.

The look on Jeff's face was one of pure happiness. Caroline and Jeff played together until it was time to go. The social workers closed the conference by making available a stack of applications on the table. If anyone was interested in taking the next step, they could begin. Jeff stood up, walked to the table and picked up the application packet without any hesitation. Caroline had reached Jeff in a way no one else could. God had given us the nudge we were waiting for.

We drove home from the workshop in a peaceful silence. Jeff's face showed confidence and serenity about our decision to move forward. I sat watching the road blur by and began to plan. I felt energized about our decision, but there was a lot to do. It would be a long process, but I knew we were ready.

◆   ◆   ◆

It seemed appropriate to talk to family and friends about our decision.

"We're going to adopt a little girl from China," I announced over dinner with my parents.

"That's great," my mother replied mildly. "Congratulations!" Her reaction was neither excited nor disappointed. I don't think my Dad looked up from his meal.

They weren't completely surprised because I had spoken before about adopting. My parents don't usually become outwardly excited about things. Even if I announced I won a million dollars, I wouldn't expect them to jump up and down. My father would quickly warn me about the tax consequences and urge me to contact an attorney. Although I wished they shared our passion, I knew things would change once the baby arrived.

Jeff's mother was surprised and overjoyed about our adoption plans. She handled it very well considering she was unprepared for the announcement. She asked many questions and seemed satisfied with Jeff's answers.

Most reactions were positive and enthusiastic. There were many personal questions asked. The questions usually started with, "Can't you have children of your own?" Most people assume adoption is a second choice, decided only after it's discovered that biological children are not an option. No matter how hard I tried, I wasn't able to articulate why we preferred to adopt rather than making our own. To tell someone it was a "feeling" we had and we wanted to provide a home to a child who needed one didn't seem to satisfy people's curiosity. This wasn't a selfless act on our part, nor an act of humanitarianism. We were ready to be parents, and our daughter was in China.

The other frequently asked question was, "Why China? Why not adopt one of our own?" "One of our own" seemed to imply that a Caucasian child needing a home in the country of our residence was more deserving than a child living somewhere else. In reality, a child living in our country who needs a family is still provided with healthcare, education, nourishing food, clean water and a place to live. What kind of life does an orphaned child have in a third world country?

After I received the same questions over and over again, I realized a lot of people had similar feelings and concerns about adopting from China. I decided to prepare an information packet about the situation in China, our decision and what the adoption process would entail. I sent the packet to interested family and friends and hoped it would answer some of their questions. I received an overwhelmingly positive response, and the explanations seemed to settle some of the unspoken uneasiness.

Paper Chasing

○ ○

A gem is not polished without friction,
not a person perfected without trials.

——*Confucius*

The application packet we picked up from the conference was actually a pre-application. Dillon International doles out the paperwork assignments one at a time to help families think seriously about adopting and to keep them from becoming overwhelmed with the paperwork.

The pre-application questions were thought provoking and helped spark some discussions of our feelings about being parents. The application asked us why we were interested in adopting and why specifically adopting internationally. What were our feelings on being an interracial family, how would friends and family react to a Chinese child, and how would we deal with racism? These were heavy questions.

We anticipated that family and friends would be very supportive of our decision and we were secure in our feeling that our daughter would be welcomed with open arms. The questions prompted me to think about how our child would be treated at school and in public. Would other kids tease her and make insulting gestures mimicking her eyes? Would strangers not talk to her thinking she didn't speak English? Would she feel different and out of place?

It made me remember my own childhood and how other kids would tease me about my red hair and big feet. I hated my hair and wore shoes many sizes too small in an attempt to conceal my foot length. I felt self-conscious about anything I wore that might draw attention to my feet, or any colors that might showcase my red hair. After years of wearing shoes too small, my feet showed signs of trauma from being "bound." I finally had no choice but to wear my true shoe size, a size twelve, and today couldn't care less how big they look. I'm grateful for my red curly hair. I feel lucky every morning when I do virtually nothing to style it.

Every child feels out of place about something and must learn to deal with and appreciate her unique differences. Would our daughter experience similar fears and anxieties which ultimately weren't vastly different from my own? But how could I compare racism to being teased about hair color? It would be important for us to be sensitive to her feelings and keep conversations open about being an Asian-American adoptee. Raising a child, whether biological or adopted, requires a great deal of understanding and attention.

At the end of October 1999, two weeks after the Dillon International workshop, we mailed our pre-application packet and waited for a response. Within a week, we received our official application packet.

"It's here!" I shouted to Jeff holding the brown envelope with Dillon International's logo on it.

I anxiously opened it and read the steps that would be required next. This was the beginning of what is not so affectionately called the "paper chase." It isn't a hard process but is certainly very detailed and not for the disorganized. I created file folders and detailed to-do lists to keep track of every document and procedure. There were three phases of paperwork we needed to complete: applications to the Immigration and Naturalization Service; applications necessary for our adoption agency; and a dossier to be submitted to the Chinese government.

The first step was to pre-file with the Immigration and Naturalization Service, or INS. The pre-filing begins the process of bringing the child into the United States. INS approval can take many months, so it was important to get this going right away. We filled out the appropriate form and included copies of our birth certificates, marriage license, a cover letter and a check.

About four weeks after mailing our documents, we received an appointment letter to be fingerprinted at the INS office in Oklahoma City. Our fingerprints would be mailed to the FBI for a criminal background check. Jeff and I made the hour-and-a-half drive to Oklahoma City in bitter cold weather, over icy roads. Jeff had to pump gas into the car before we reached the INS office and ended up spilling gas on his hands. As we tried to clean his hands, we noticed how dry and cracked they became from the gas and the cold air. I had read stories about families who were fingerprinted, and the prints weren't readable. Too much hand lotion or overly dry hands produce poor prints. It took months for the unreadable prints to be noticed, and it slowed the process down considerably. Those families had to be fingerprinted again months later.

At the INS office, we waited in a room filled with people who had emigrated from other countries. It was an interesting mix of nationalities and languages. A very serious but kind officer took us to the fingerprinting area. In the movies, the criminals are often shown being fingerprinted by rolling each finger in the inkpad, but according to our officer, this isn't how to get a good print. We simply pressed each finger directly in the inkpad and stamped it on the paper. We felt fortunate our INS officer seemed to know what she was doing. In spite of Jeff's dry, gas stained hands, his prints turned out clear and perfect.

The formal application required by our adoption agency wasn't difficult but it took two months to complete. We filled out a lengthy form providing answers to questions about our jobs, education, history, marriage, finances, and a list of five references. Dillon International would contact each reference and ask them many questions about us.

"Who do you think we should list as references?" I asked as I grabbed our address book and flipped through the names for ideas.

Jeff looked through the list with me. "They need to be people who know us both very well." We chose three couples, and our best friends from childhood. It was important to choose articulate people who would give us favorable reviews.

In addition to the application, we had to provide statements about our health, documentation of our financial status, a letter from our health insurance provider stating coverage would be provided to an adopted child, and letters from our employers listing our annual salaries. We needed a certified letter from the local sheriff's department stating we did not have criminal records, certified copies of our birth certificates and marriage license, copies of our passports, copies of our income tax returns, and pictures of ourselves and our home.

"Adopting isn't easy," I complained to Jeff as I organized the paperwork. "You really have to be serious about being a parent to go through this much work."

"If conceiving a child was this involved, there might not be as many unwanted, abused children in our society," Jeff commented as he glanced over the lengthy list of adoption requirements.

In our early thirties, we were considered young to be adopting from China, but were fortunate that the age minimum had recently been lowered from thirty-five to thirty. We found that most adoptive parents are in their forties. At the time, China generally placed younger children with younger parents, and older children with the older parents. We requested to adopt a healthy girl less than nine months of age. We anticipated receiving a referral of a baby around six months old.

A referral is made when the dossier paperwork is matched with the paperwork of a baby available for adoption. The China Center for Adoption Affairs makes the match and then sends the adoption agency a picture and current information about the baby. The agency contacts the family with the referral. Occasionally a family declines the referral. If the child is older than requested, has medical problems the family doesn't feel comfortable accepting, or the match doesn't feel right, they may ask for the assignment of another child. Ideally, as much information as possible is provided, but with China, there is limited information available. The referral does include weight, height, medical information, and sometimes personality traits and developmental milestones. The information may or may not be accurate.

We filled out a lengthy list of health conditions we would and would not accept. Would we accept a child with a cleft palate? Sight or hearing impaired? Physical deformity? AIDS? I found it very uncomfortable answering these questions.

"What about a child with mental retardation?" Jeff asked looking at me blankly. "Are we prepared to take on that kind of responsibility?"

"If we were giving birth to a child, these decisions would be in God's hands," I replied to Jeff, feeling very uncomfortable with the question. "What if the daughter meant for us has one of these conditions? Who are we to pick and choose?" We answered each question with our gut instinct and went on to the next form.

We were each asked to write a detailed autobiography, including our feelings about our childhood, education, family, professions, interests, and thoughts about becoming parents. I wrote my own autobiography within two hours without much difficulty. It was relatively painless as the words seemed to flow naturally. Jeff, on the other hand, had never given much thought to how he "felt" about things. Describing his feelings was a new experience. This was a very difficult project for him. I thought he'd never complete it because each question took him hours. I'm sure this is typical with many men. He sat at the computer with his head in his hands.

"This is hard! I don't know what I feel!" he shouted with frustration from the computer room.

Jeff finally completed his autobiography after nearly fifteen hours of work. I was very proud and relieved. We submitted our documents to Dillon International in January of 2000 and were approved within days.

Once approved, we could begin our home study. For the home study, a social worker visits the prospective parents' home to learn more about the family. This helps to ensure that they will provide a good home for a child.

An appointment was set with our assigned social worker, Rebecca from Dillon International. We didn't worry about the meeting and didn't put a lot of work into cleaning up the house. We thought we'd put it off until the last minute.

The weekend before our Monday meeting with Rebecca, some old friends offered us a free trip to Las Vegas. Our friends were going with a group, and two people had to cancel at the last minute. We were offered their tickets, and naturally, we couldn't pass up a free trip, so we left the next day.

We arrived home late Sunday night with only a few hours left to clean and get ready for the meeting the next day. Many families clean their houses impeccably before the social worker arrives, but we barely got the kitchen counters cleaned off and the dog hair off the couch. She would certainly see our house in its natural state. I was surprisingly calm and confident everything would go smoothly.

Our social worker was very easy to talk to, and we enjoyed the meeting. She asked us more detailed questions about things we had discussed in our autobiographies, and we talked a lot about our philosophies on raising children. We discussed discipline, racism, and being an interracial family. She recommended some good books on adoption and child rearing, which we later read. We had two additional meetings with her individually at which Jeff and I discussed our feelings about each other. We felt grateful to have her share this experience with us and knew she'd be helpful and supportive even after we brought our daughter home.

The third step of the adoption process, which I feel was the most annoying, was preparing the dossier. The dossier is the group of documents required by the People's Republic of China to apply for adopting a child. The process is exhausting because in our state each document must be stamped by a notary, certified by the county and state, and then sent to the Chinese Consulate to be stamped. Each certifies the legitimacy of the "seal" affixed by the previous level. The documents are properly certified at each level so that the Chinese government is confident the original documents are authentic. For example, one of the required documents was a letter of employment from my employer. I was first required to have the letter notarized by a notary public. Then, I had to take that document to the county courthouse to have the court clerk certify that the notary who notarized the document was a certified notary. Next, the document had to be sent to our Secretary of State to verify the notary was indeed licensed in the state. And finally, the document had to be sent to the Chinese Consulate, located in Houston, Texas, which had jurisdiction over our state. The Chinese Consulate authenticates the document attached by our Secretary of State. So one notarized letter of employment had three pieces of paper stapled to it!

This process had to be completed for each document submitted to China, and we were charged a fee every time it was done. Documents required for the dossier included a letter of application, a copy of our home study, certified copies of our birth certificates and marriage license. Letters of employment, financial statements, and copies of our passport were needed, along with letters from our local police department stating we had no criminal records. We received our INS approval to adopt and this document needed to be included as well.

We had to undergo a complete physical examination. We were examined, tested for various diseases, questioned about our medical history, fertility status, and overall health. A complete list of all medications and reasons why we needed them had to be included in the written report. Every question had to be answered and signed by our physician.

After we gathered all these documents, we began the "stamping" process. The documents were notarized and I took them to our county courthouse to be certified. I "overnighted" them to Oklahoma City, our state capital, to be state certified and included an additional overnight envelope for them to be returned. Once they were returned, I "overnighted" them to the Chinese Consulate in Houston and again provided an overnight envelope for their return. The fees ranged from $5 to $30 per stamp per document depending on where they were stamped.

After the Chinese Consulate returned the documents, I proofread them one more time for any errors. The slightest inaccuracy could cause our paperwork to be returned by the Chinese government. I checked and double-checked and finally felt confident that our paperwork was ready to take to Dillon International. It took six months for us to collect and have certified all the documentation for the INS, home study and dossier.

The paperwork process was an expensive part of the adoption journey. In fact, it cost us more than $8,000 to complete the paperwork required by our government and the Chinese government just to apply for the adoption. With health exams, document fees, agency fees, expedited shipping, home study costs and document stamping, expenses added up quickly. When adopting internationally, many people assume most of the fees go to the child's country of origin, but this is not necessarily the case. Once in China, an orphanage donation is made and there are some paperwork fees, but China receives very little of the total cost to adopt. China requires the parents to travel to the country to receive the child. They may benefit from our tourism dollars, with airfare, accommodations, meals and tours, but most of the expenses are incurred in the United States.

I carefully made five photocopies of each document in our dossier including the documentation attached to each one of them. It was a tedious task as I spent over two hours carefully copying each page. I carried the completed stack in my arms and pressed my chin on top to keep it from toppling over. It was a lot of paper. I delivered the original and a copy to the Dillon International office. Dillon International tries to send dossiers to China in groups of three or more. The dossiers are grouped together and assigned referrals at the same time. The families of the dossiers grouped together will likely receive referrals in the same area of China and can travel together as a group.

As I left the documents at the front desk, I felt there should be a celebration for reaching this final step.

"Shouldn't there be noise makers, confetti, and streamers?" I teased the receptionist.

I felt exhilarated, proud and excited. What a labor of love to prepare this stack of paperwork that would eventually be matched with our daughter's paperwork in China. We were now "paperwork pregnant."

The Wait

If happiness is in your destiny, you need not be in a hurry.

——*Chinese proverb*

Our dossier was mailed to China in May of 2000, and the wait for a referral began. Our dossier was sent with the dossiers of five other families. We were already good friends with three of the families. Chuck and Dana were the family we saw arrive home with their daughter, Caroline. Now they were waiting for their second daughter, soon to be Susanna, and we looked forward to traveling with them. Steve and Cheryl traveled to China with Chuck and Dana for their first daughter, Emily, and now would be with them again to bring home Annie. Steve and Charlene also had a daughter from China, Lauren, and would welcome their new little girl, Isabella. I felt relieved we would be in such good company. As a new parent, I welcomed their experience.

At the time we sent our dossier, it was taking the Chinese officials approximately eight to nine months to send a referral to waiting families. Using that timeframe, we anticipated receiving news of our daughter by Christmas. It would make a wonderful gift!

The first few months of the wait went by quickly. We busily completed home remodeling projects and prepared for our new arrival. We did a major overhaul to our house, knowing full well there wouldn't be time or energy to tackle such projects when the baby came. We sanded hardwood floors, replaced carpet and flooring, and made annoying but necessary repairs. We turned our extra bedroom into an adorable nursery decorated in gingham and flowers. The walls were pistachio green with soft yellow shades and blue gingham valances. I stenciled little flowers along the wall to make the room feel cozy and inviting.

"Look at this gorgeous toy chest," I said to Jeff as I pointed to a picture in the Pottery Barn catalogue. "This would go perfectly in the baby room!"

"Yeah, it's beautiful all right, but look at that price." Jeff didn't share my enthusiasm for baby décor.

"Well, why don't you build one then? Can you build a toy chest to look like this?" I handed him the catalogue to get a closer look.

"Yup," he answered very confidently, "just tell me how big you want it and I can build it." And he did. Jeff built a beautiful toy chest almost exactly like the one in the catalogue for a third of the price. I painted it to match the room and added my stenciled flowers. On the bottom of the chest, Jeff wrote a special message to our forthcoming daughter we had lovingly decided to name "Adelynn" and glued a 2001 penny. It was his first creation for his baby girl.

The Internet was a constant source of support and information. One website, the Families with Children from China[9] site, was particularly helpful. It was a wealth of information for every stage of the entire adoption process. I kept a close eye on the Chinese adoptive parents' message boards, checking for the latest status of referrals arriving for other waiting families.

The date our paperwork was sent to China is informally referred to as one's DTC or "dossier to China." The DTC establishes the date when your paperwork was sent and helps track referral times. There was an email list community made up of other families who sent their paperwork to China at the same time as ours, a friendship of strangers all experiencing similar frustrations, anticipation and anxieties. It provided a wealth of information with tips on what to pack, what to wear, what books to read and general gossip about when referrals might arrive. We could monitor when the families before our DTC date had received referrals.

Just for fun and to add to the enthusiasm, the waiting Internet families held their own Internet baby shower. I cross-stitched a teddy bear dressed in a beautiful beaded Chinese silk dress for the family we were assigned. I was so happy with how it turned out that I made another one for our baby room. We received from our Internet family some needed items like socks, spoons, toys, and a baby's picture book, which we filled with family photos and pictures of our dogs. These were the first baby gifts we received. It was fun opening each gift and creating a place to put them. As I pulled the newly washed baby socks from my dryer I felt my heart race. The reality that there would be a little person in our home wearing these cute tiny socks made me both excited and a little scared.

By fall, we knew we were months away from a referral and definitely wouldn't know anything until after Christmas. It became apparent we wouldn't receive a referral until early spring. We were disappointed but glad to have some extra time to plan and prepare.

Since the process was delayed, there was time to squeeze in one more exotic vacation. It would be our last indulgent trip together, just the two of us. We discussed some possible destinations but couldn't make a decision. I was lying in bed thinking about where we should go when the thought of visiting Antarctica jumped into my head. "Can you vacation in Antarctica?" I wondered. I crept out of bed and logged onto the computer. In my email mailbox was a budget travel newsletter. Clicking on the file, the first line of the newsletter read, "Chilling Antarctica—An Affordable Tour." I blinked my eyes in disbelief. Another trip we were destined to take!

Jeff and I booked the tour, and I prepared for the trip. I quickly discovered properly insulated outdoor clothing required for Antarctica weather was very expensive. It didn't make sense for us to spend a lot of money on clothing we would never use again. Applying my bargain hunter skills, I found a website selling discounted hunter's clothing. I ordered a down, waterproof jacket, overalls and gloves in each of our sizes. The prices were unbelievable, but the drawback was that they were bright, neon orange.

"Hey Dad, check out our Antarctica gear," I called as I pulled out our recently shipped purchases for him to inspect.

"Bright!" He exclaimed, grimacing at the orange clothing. "If you fall overboard they won't have any trouble finding you," he joked.

"Dad, if I fall overboard I'll probably die on contact when I hit the freezing water." I laughed but saw my mom's face flush pale.

We made many long flights to reach the southern tip of South America, traveling from Tulsa to Atlanta, Miami, Buenos Aires and finally to Ushuaia. There we boarded a Russian cargo ship converted for passengers. The ship was large enough for 125 people but too small to soften the slapping of the high seas. As the ship crossed the Drake Passage it became impossible to walk about the ship. Jeff tried to steady me, but he didn't have the strength to hold us both up. My long legs were less than seaworthy leaving me staggering down the ship corridor like a drunken Great Dane puppy. Seasickness is a dreadful thing, especially trapped in less than luxurious conditions for nine days. We slept on bunk beds, complete with safety belts to keep sleeping passengers from rolling out of bed. Once the ship anchored, I felt fine. We climbed into zodiacs (small inflatable rafts) and trolled around icebergs observing penguin rookeries. We triumphantly landed on the continent of Antarctica.

"We're here," I cheered stepping on land in my knee-high waders.

"Hey, a chinstrap penguin," Jeff announced pointing to a baby waddling our way. Being unaffected by seasickness, he attended the educational seminars being held on the ship. The penguins toddled around, bumping into rocks, and flipping over other penguins. We quietly laughed, trying not to scare them.

"I could sit here for hours," I whispered to Jeff who was sitting on a rock beside me.

"Cute little things, aren't they?" Jeff laughed again seeing a fuzzy baby waddling after its momma.

Even my restless stomach couldn't spoil the experience. What a glorious last adventure before becoming parents!

◆   ◆   ◆

Once back in the states, parenting preparations resumed. We volunteered in our church nursery to get ourselves accustomed to diaper changing and childcare. The nursery director knew we were novices and started us out with rocking the little babies. We would rock and wonder what it would be like to hold our own little girl. As we gained some experience, we graduated to diaper changing and potty chair assistance.

"Do I have to wipe their bottoms after they use the potty chair?" Jeff asked with an unpleasant look on his face. "Can't they do that themselves?"

"No, Mr. Woodard, I'm afraid at this age they'll need some help," said the nursery school director as she smiled and looked at me.

"I'll wipe the girls, but you're in charge of the boys," I announced before realizing most of the nursery was filled with little girls.

Jeff managed to avoid the "wiping" altogether and had some difficultly changing the diapers. If they weren't on backwards, they wouldn't be fastened properly and would droop off during play. He eventually specialized in just playing with the kids, which both he and the children loved. The little girls loved to have tea parties with him and put silly bows in his hair.

One little girl in particular, Claire, captured our hearts. She herself was adopted from China and made volunteering at the nursery a joy. Very intelligent, she always had something interesting to say.

"Miss Sarah, why is your hair all curly and red?" she asked with an inquisitive look on her face.

"Well, Claire, I don't know why," I replied, not really knowing what to say.

"That's just how God made you?" she asked with her beautiful dark eyes gazing at me intently.

"Yup, that's just how God made me." She nodded, satisfied with her own explanation and went back to playing.

She had a wonderful sense of humor and loved to sing The Backstreet Boys songs while she played with the pretend kitchen.

"Ah you pee-pee cashew see, cashew see" she'd sing for the lyrics "All you people can't you see, can't you see."

We laughed, and enjoyed her immensely.

During the wait, I spent a great deal of time educating myself about possible medical and emotional issues our daughter might face. As with giving birth to a child, there are always risks and concerns. The biggest fear many people have about adopting is the attachment issue. To what extent will the child be emotionally affected from being institutionalized? Attachment disorders sometimes occur when a child has not developed a secure relationship with a caregiver.[10] There has been some scary information publicized about attachment problems in adopted children. Whether or not the child has a problem attaching to the new adoptive parents depends a lot on the child, her past experiences, and what the new parents do to enhance attachment. It was a challenge we were prepared to confront.

I eagerly learned about the many things parents can do to help promote attachment and bonding when they receive their new child. Having skin-to-skin contact with the baby by snuggling together, bathing, dancing or swimming helps enhance attachment. Direct eye contact is very important. Playing games like peek-a-boo, giving Eskimo kisses and playing the "Where's my nose?" game help encourage eye contact. Bottle time provides a great opportunity to nurture and bond. I learned that close cuddling, strong eye contact, and holding the bottle for the baby sends the message of trust and security. Another great suggestion I read on the adoptive family email list, was to do baby massage. Gently rubbing lotion on the baby's body and letting her watch in the mirror helps the baby see her parents caring for and loving her. These were just a few suggestions we intended to integrate into our daily routine with our daughter. We hoped these techniques would help her feel comfortable and learn to trust us. We would do whatever we could to make her transition as easy as possible.

I tried to prepare myself for parenthood in every possible way. I read books about how to explain the adoption story to our child, books to help our daughter cope with being adopted, and books about being an interracial family. I studied discipline, discrimination, and baby how-to manuals. Jeff and I participated in Chinese cultural events and avidly watched anything airing on television about China. We took CPR for adults, CPR for children, and attended parenting classes. We introduced our three dogs, Marcie, a Shar-pei, Andrew, a giant Lab/Dalmatian mix, and Jacob, a Shepherd/Collie mix, to children on a regular basis. We practiced tugging their hair and putting our hands in their food bowls to prepare them for the small child who would be arriving soon.[11] They soon became "childproofed" and we felt confident in their gentleness.

Jeff and I made it a point to focus a lot of energy on each other. We had a strong marriage and we wanted to maintain that special bond when the baby arrived. I knew too many couples who weren't able to sustain their marriage through parenthood. Nurturing my relationship with Jeff would require love and attention, just like the new baby. Jeff and I were best friends. That friendship started the first time we met.

Jeff and I met under amusing circumstances. We were introduced by mutual friends. These friends were also advertising clients of mine and avid square dancers. They called one day and asked, "Sarah, why don't you take square dance lessons with us?"

"Square dance lessons?" I tried to hide the disgust in my voice.

I wanted nothing of it. The idea of parading around in one of those silly skirts had absolutely no appeal to me. But they were a delightful couple. I didn't want to disappoint them, so I bargained.

"Okay, I'll do it if you can find a thirty-year-old hunk for my dance partner." I consented, assuming a good-looking thirty-year-old man who could square dance did not exist. I dismissed it from my mind.

Within a few weeks, they called to announce they found my hunk. No doubt a short, dumpy man, wearing light orange polyester pants and cockroach-killer boots. I fumbled with some excuses, but they were determined and too sweet to turn down.

As promised, I arrived at the dance hall. There wasn't a soul in the building under fifty years old. I looked around in fear. Just as I began to feel that "Jeff" might not show, in walked my dance partner. Much to my amazement, my hunk was actually quite hunky. Tall, dark hair, dark eyes, tan, employed and not living with his mother! A dream come true.

We exchanged some light chatter about our friends who had arranged our meeting. I confided in him my loathing of taking square dance lessons.

"It's really kinda fun," he laughed. "Give it a try, just tonight."

The music started, and the caller chanted instructions. Jeff was an advanced square dancer. I could dance, but the "swing your partner" stuff was out of my league. I awkwardly mimicked Jeff's dance steps. We roared with laughter as I stepped on his feet and crashed into the other dancers. We spent a silly night do-se-do-ing, and the rest is history. Square dancing was a one-time adventure for me, but the crazy decision to go opened up a life-time of adventures together. Jeff has been my closest friend ever since. Our decision to become parents added even more depth to our relationship.

During the long wait for our referral, I would lie in bed at night and think about where our daughter might be. Was she born yet? Was someone holding and feeding her? Was she sick? If our daughter was still in her birth mother's womb, I prayed the mother had enough to eat and was taking care of herself. I thought about where our daughter might be born.

"Who do you think will cut the umbilical cord?" I whispered to Jeff just before he fell sleep.

"I don't know, honey," he responded, knowing I wouldn't be sleeping again that night.

I prayed that if our daughter was in the orphanage, she was being held, cared for, and loved. Fearfully, I envisioned a little girl sitting in a crib sobbing continually with no one responding. I prayed that God would let our daughter feel our love all the way from Oklahoma and know we were on our way.

It was now spring of 2001. Many months went by, and it seemed we would never receive the referral of our daughter. Anxious friends and family were constantly asking us when the baby would be here. We appreciated their genuine interest but it was difficult to say over and over, "I don't know. Soon, I hope." I kept a watchful eye on the Internet message boards, and knew the time was getting close. At one point, families who sent their paperwork at the same time we did received their referrals. We waited and waited but heard nothing. Our adoption agency contacted the officials in China and discovered our paperwork had been misplaced in the Chinese offices. We would be set back an additional two months. This additional delay meant our paperwork was close to expiring. If the wait continued, we would be forced to re-do our paperwork with all the expenses that go along with it. Waiting for our daughter was difficult enough without the looming paperwork expiration. It was an emotional roller coaster I never imagined we'd ride.

The dossiers were finally reviewed and errors were found in two of the dossiers submitted. The paperwork was returned to those families for correction. One of the families was Chuck and Dana. Three lines of information were not filled out correctly on their medical report. The paperwork would need to be redone and returned to the officials in China. Because of this delay, they would not travel in our group. We were heartbroken. We had looked forward to having these friends with us during this important journey. It was disappointing to us, and even more upsetting to Chuck and Dana. They corrected their documents and quickly returned them to the officials in China.

From the beginning of our decision to adopt, we planned that I would leave my job to stay home with our daughter. In addition to my job in advertising sales, I did voice-over production, voicing radio and television commercials. I intended to continue doing voice work part-time, but knew business would be sporadic.

"I think we can live comfortably on one income, but we'll need to make a few lifestyle changes," I told Jeff as I reviewed my proposed budget. "If we can eliminate one of our car payments we'll be in good shape."

We sold Jeff's Jeep Grand Cherokee and bought my dad's old farm truck. Although it was beaten up, my dad has always maintained vehicles by the book, so mechanically it was well cared for. We actually enjoyed cleaning it up. I helped shampoo the seats and clean the interior. Jeff can fix anything, so he repaired what needed attention and waxed the exterior. From a distance, our little truck with over 170,000 miles looked pretty good. By subtracting the car payment, full insurance coverage on a new vehicle, and gas on an SUV, this one simple change saved us almost $600 a month. Instead of feeling embarrassed driving an old truck, Jeff felt proud. It was a small sacrifice to make so that I could be home with our daughter full-time.

We saved money in other ways by continuing to live in our small, comfortable house.

"Once that baby gets here," friends would warn us, "you'll wish you had a bigger house."

With less than 1,100 square feet, our house would be cozy with two adults, three large dogs and a baby. But our $550 house payment with only ten years remaining on the loan was too smart an arrangement to give up. According to our budget, with smarter shopping, eating out less and downsizing, we could still live comfortably on Jeff's income.

Knowing our dossier was "in the system," I gave my resignation. It wasn't as hard as I feared it would be. I was scared about losing my sense of independence but was ready for my next challenge. I knew I was doing the right thing.

My dear friend, Eileen, had planned for almost a year to host my baby shower. She was in the process of buying and selling a home. Setting a date to have my shower was becoming awkward. The wait continued on and on with no referral.

"Depending on when your referral arrives," Eileen worried, "I may be in the middle of moving." We knew we were getting close so we decided to go ahead with the baby shower. At least we'd have the big items needed for when the baby arrived.

Without knowing the age of our daughter, we registered for the essentials. There is so much to buy for a new baby that it was easy to build a lengthy list of supplies. My friends held a wonderful shower for me. The cake was decorated with a colorful Chinese flag, and there were other "Chinese touches" to add to the festivities. Among many nice gifts, Dana gave me a beautiful jeweled frame for our referral picture and a sprig of bamboo. Today, the stalk of bamboo is almost six feet high. I hope to pass on the tradition and give a cutting of it to another waiting family someday. We received all the things we'd need. We managed to cram a car seat, high chair, monitor, clothing, books, frames, fuzzy animals and other goodies into my car. I was thrilled and touched that my friends and family were so thoughtful and generous. The shower was fun, and preparing a place to put our gifts made things seem more real.

Our Referral

A smile will gain you ten more years of life.

——*Chinese proverb*

In late May of 2001, almost thirteen months after our paperwork was sent to China, we received rumors through the Internet grapevine. A batch of referrals had been mailed from the translator's office in China and sent to their respective adoption agencies. The only way to know if our adoption agency made the list was to find out if a package was on its way. My friend Charlene and I were determined to get some answers. We made inquiring calls to the various shipping companies to track any packages that might be leaving from Beijing, China and heading to Tulsa. We called every express shipping company that ships from China and explained our situation. We were lucky to speak to some empathetic customer service agents.

"This isn't just any package arriving from China," I gently explained. "This is a package containing the pictures and information of five baby girls waiting for their parents!"

"Oh, how wonderful!" a thoughtful customer service agent replied. "Let's see if we can locate your girls."

By giving them the destination zip code, they could do a search in their system. After a few calls, we determined there was, in fact, a package heading our way. We were thrilled! We obtained the tracking number and spent the next few days tracking its progress on the Internet. I became obsessed with tracking the package and would enter the tracking number almost on the hour to see if it had moved.

Normally, I'm a levelheaded person who stays emotionally grounded and looks at things logically. The eighteen months of paperwork, waiting, and anticipation had finally cracked me. There was so little about the process that we had any control over. Our fate had been in the hands of the Chinese government for so long. Knowing the package of referrals was really on its way made me very excited and anxious. I'd wake up in the middle of the night, log on, and check to see where the package was. I could see where the package was scanned in San Francisco, and bound for Memphis. Memphis seemed a bit out of the way for my liking, but I didn't have any say in the flight plan. The wait was becoming physically painful as my stomach burned from stressful anticipation. Monday was Memorial Day, so our precious package would be left sitting and waiting another day.

Early on Tuesday morning, my Internet tracking frenzy started again, and I watched with amazement as the package left Memphis and entered Tulsa's facility. I hit "refresh" on my computer and watched the package's progress change before my eyes. Within minutes, I saw where a representative from our adoption agency signed for the package. With wide eyes I looked again to make sure what I saw was real. I jumped up and down screaming, "Oh, my God!" over and over. I grabbed the phone and called Jeff at work.

"It's here!" I shouted. "Our referral is here! Dillon just signed for it!"

Jeff left his office and I left the house to meet at Dillon International's office to see the long awaited picture of our daughter. I called my waiting friend Charlene to make sure she knew the referrals were in, but she was way ahead of me. She and her husband were on their way, too.

Jeff and I arrived at Dillon International's office at about the same time. It was just before nine in the morning. We walked up the stairs together, and I became breathless from the short climb. My excitement had me breathing fast and hard. We walked in and were led to our social worker's office. We were nervous and giddy. From down the hall, we heard shrieks of joy as Charlene and Steve were viewing for the first time the picture of their little girl.

Our social worker, Rebecca, pulled some papers out of a large manila envelope and asked us to be seated. She studied the papers and appeared cautious. As a professional social worker, she handled the presentation of our referral with great care. She said the girl referred to us was older than we requested. Jeff and I both gulped. We asked to be assigned a baby less than nine months old. She explained this girl was 10 ½ months old, named Ji Chen Ge, and was residing in the Jian City Welfare Institute in the Jiangxi Province of China.

"Okay," I was thinking, "10 ½ months isn't much older. I can deal with that."

She then mentioned the little girl had a red mark under her eye. My heart sank. Biting on my thumbnail, I silently worried. Was there something seriously wrong with the baby?

Rebecca reassured us, but wanted us to be fully informed. She handed us three pictures. Jeff and I were stunned. We just held the pictures and stared. We didn't react like Charlene and her husband did. We were thrown into serious shock. Both of us. I was surprised I didn't immediately feel any maternal instincts towards the picture, or instant love. Many people do when they first see their referral photos.

She was a tiny girl with a sweet smile and beautiful eyes. She seemed serious and alert. The pictures appeared to have been taken when she was maybe three months old. She wore black tights and a dress two sizes too big for her. Her black wispy hair stood straight up on her head. She had a small red welt under her right eye, like she might have scratched herself, or maybe, had pink eye. It didn't look to be anything serious, but we couldn't be sure. In the picture she held her head up and had her fists clenched. This seemed like a good sign. It appeared she had some strength and could support herself. I tried to envision myself holding this little girl. It was a strange feeling to instantly become a mother to a little girl in a picture. Jeff and I silently held the picture. This was our daughter.

We anxiously read the paperwork giving what little information was known about her. It was written in Chinese on very thin pieces of paper. Attached to each paper was an English translation. It stated she was found in the waiting room of a bus station when she was only three days old. Many abandoned children are found with no information regarding their birth date, so the orphanage must guess. We were fortunate that a note with her birth date was written on a piece of red paper and left with her. In China, the color red symbolizes good luck. No information was available about her birthparents. We assume she was abandoned because of the one child policy, but we'll never know for sure.

The orphanage director named her Ji Chen Ge. In China, the last name is listed first. So her first name was Chen, middle name was Ge, and last name was Ji. Ji represents Jian, the city where she was found. Chen is the year she was born, the year of the dragon, and Ge because the director thought she was very pretty. Her nickname was Lao Shu, meaning Mouse, because she was quick, small, and very flexible.

The paperwork included a medical exam summary and progress report given nine months earlier. The medical exam results and progress report seemed rather generic and were not current. Everything on the medical report was listed as normal and her progress report showed her to be developmentally on track. We could only go on blind faith that everything was correct. She appeared to be a healthy little girl. Rebecca asked us to take the information home and take our time making our decision as to whether or not we would accept this referral or request another. She recommended we have a pediatrician review the medical report. Of course we would accept the referral, but it was nice to have some time to adjust. We had waited so long, and now had a picture of our daughter waiting for us in China. It was overwhelming.

We left the agency, both feeling a little stunned and nervous. We immediately went to make color copies of the pictures because we wanted to preserve the originals. We made enough copies to give to family and friends. We felt ourselves building with excitement as the copier hummed and presented our freshly printed color photos. These pictures were of our daughter. OUR DAUGHTER! The reality was scary and exhilarating.

It was raining when we were finished making our copies, so I carefully covered the precious manila envelope under my coat as we ran back to our cars. Jeff jumped into my car and pulled out a beautifully wrapped box.

"Here," he whispered, pulling a little package from under his raincoat," I've been waiting to give this to you."

I opened the box and pulled out the protective Styrofoam wrapping. Inside was a Boyd's Bear figurine of a momma bear and daddy bear, holding a cute baby girl bear.[12] In the daddy bear's back pocket is a tiny book reading, "Parenting 101." And written at the bottom, "Love makes a couple…And baby makes a family."

"Oh, Jeff!" I cried. I was overwhelmed with emotion. I burst into tears and we held each other for a long time. I'm not sure who cried harder. Jeff bought the special figurine months ago and waited for our referral day to present it to me. It was a real-life Hallmark commercial.

Jeff went back to work and I sat in my car in the parking lot. I continued to look at the pictures as the rain beat down on the roof of the car. I couldn't take my eyes off the pictures to drive home. My hair was damp from the rain, and the windows were fogging up. The memory is very vivid. Ji Chen Ge looked sad in the pictures, I thought. Our little girl was so far away from us and desperately needed to come home. I could physically feel my maternal instincts kicking in and I ached at the thought of not being there for her. I worried she didn't have enough to eat, was neglected, or felt unwanted. I became nauseous. My daughter needed me and I had to get there fast. At that very moment, I became a mom.

All the waiting families in our group turned in the acceptance paperwork within a day of receiving the referrals. We shared in each other's excitement. We emailed each other the pictures of our new daughters. Two of the families received referrals for baby girls at the same orphanage where our daughter resided. Sadly, all three babies were wearing the same dress in their referral pictures. It must have been the "good dress" they reserved for picture taking.

Some additional paperwork was required. We had to wait for travel approval, which the China Center for Adoption Affairs issues after acceptance documents are received and forwarded to the orphanage. Then we could get an appointment with the United States Consulate in Guangzhou, China. The U.S. Consulate appointment is the last step of paperwork required which would enable us to leave China with our daughter. Once we had our appointment, we could make arrangements to travel. Things would move quickly once the appointment was set.

On the Internet, I located other families who had adopted from our daughter's orphanage. Based on their information, I learned that our daughter would be brought to our hotel in China, so we would be unable to visit, or even to see, the orphanage. The orphanage where our daughter resided was in a rural area far from any major city. The girls would be transported with nannies by bus to our hotel and then turned over to us. I wanted more information about the orphanage as I felt it was important for our own understanding and for our daughter's when she grew older. It would provide us with information about where and how she spent her first year of life. Through the Internet, I was able to obtain the address of the orphanage. I mailed the orphanage a care package that included a disposable camera with a picture of our daughter and her name written in Chinese taped to the back. From a family who had previously adopted from China, I obtained a letter written in Chinese asking the orphanage director to please take pictures of our daughter, Ji Chen Ge. We asked them to take pictures of the orphanage and where our daughter slept and played. I included some snacks, bath products and lotions for the caregivers, and a few baby things. I knew Ji Chen Ge would probably never see the baby items but hoped the gifts would motivate the caretakers into taking the pictures. We asked that they bring the camera when they delivered Ji Chen Ge to our hotel in China. I knew we'd be lucky if the package ever made it to the orphanage, and even luckier if someone was kind enough to take the pictures. It was worth the attempt in hopes of capturing some memories of our daughter's past.

Three weeks after our referral, the authorities in China approved our travel and Dillon International made arrangements to meet our daughter. Ji Chen Ge, soon to be Adelynn Chen-Ge Woodard, would be safely in our arms very soon. The wait was excruciating.

Journey of a Thousand Miles

○ ○

A journey of a thousand miles begins with a single step.

——*Chinese proverb*

We started the packing process for our daughter's homecoming immediately. We laid out two big suitcases in our newly decorated baby room and threw in supplies as I collected them. There was so much to take. We were advised to pack for every possible medical need.[13] The baby could have a sinus infection, constipation, diarrhea, gas, lice, scabies, allergies, or fever. Then we would need formula, bottles, bottle liners, cereal, 130 diapers, spoons, bowls, bibs, toys, clothes in various sizes, pounds of paperwork, camera, video camera, film, enough Cheerios to last two weeks, and our own clothing and toiletries. Included in our suitcase was a fabric-covered notebook I dedicated to journaling our experience. I packed body lotion and shower gel in a special fragrance I chose just for the trip. On previous vacations, I began a tradition of choosing a new scent of lotion for each trip to associate a scent with the experience. With a whiff of juniper breeze, I'm back in Russia. Hazelnut reminds me of Iran. Given as a gift, cucumber melon would be my fragrance for this memorable journey. We managed to pack everything in two giant wheeled suitcases, a medium sized suitcase and two backpacks. I still felt like we might be missing something important. We prayed the wheels wouldn't break off and our luggage would arrive in a timely fashion.

I had arranged for a China rose bush to be delivered to our house a few days before our departure date. Just hours before we left for the airport, Jeff dug a hole and planted the small, pink flowered rose in what would eventually be "Adelynn's Garden." I wanted the planting date to be the same as the day we began our journey to bring our daughter home.

"Do you think she'll like flowers?" I asked Jeff, hoping our daughter would enjoy gardening as much as we did.

"I think she will," Jeff replied as he patted down the soil with his shovel. I imagined little fingers digging through the soil and planting flowers under her special rose.

With bags packed and loaded in the car, I had a feeling of mourning as we left our house. This was the end of a chapter in our lives. I kissed and hugged our dogs, knowing our lives were going to change forever. As excited as I was, I also felt sadness. My life was good, and I was happy. We had complete freedom and a happy marriage. Was our marriage strong enough to handle the stress of a child? What would we do if she was cruel to our dogs? Would we ever get to travel again? What if our daughter had mental or emotional issues, requiring a lifetime of constant care? I feared the worst of every possible scenario but knew we would handle whatever came our way. I pushed the negative thoughts out of my mind and swallowed hard as I closed the door behind me.

Our flights from Tulsa to Los Angeles were uneventful. We flew from Los Angeles to Guangzhou, China, on China Southern Airways in their premium economy class (business class) section. China Southern has a special fare available to adopting families allowing them to fly business class for practically the cost of flying economy.[14] We were very happy with our choice to fly business class, enjoying the extra legroom, reclining seats and little extras. During the flight, we met a few other couples who were also traveling to adopt. For many, it was their first international trip and they were nervous about traveling around China. I remember how intimidating it was to arrive for the first time in a country where the people didn't speak English. We quickly adapted and enjoyed the challenge, but the initial experience was stressful. I could understand why traveling outside of the country for the first time to adopt a baby would be nerve-racking.

We landed in the People's Republic of China 15 hours later. We both slept well and arrived feeling rested and excited. Business class eases a long flight. Clearing customs was a breeze and all of our luggage arrived safely. As soon as we stepped out of Immigration we saw a tour guide holding a sign with our name on it. It was comforting to see the name "Woodard" held above the crowd. We were the only two people he was waiting for, so we quickly loaded the little minivan and the driver headed to the hotel. Guangzhou is a very congested city draped with heavy smog and teeming with thousands of people on bicycles. It was a hair-raising drive. The van darted in and out of traffic and even bumped a man on a bicycle. The tour guide continued to flip through his paperwork and didn't seem to notice. The driver was playing a Garth Brooks Greatest Hits CD as we enjoyed our views of China. I'm not sure if they played the American music to make the tourists feel at home or if it's their music of choice.

"We're from Oklahoma, just like Garth Brooks," I informed our hosts, trying to make conversation. I don't think they understood. They smiled, nodded, and kept singing along to "We Shall Be Free."

We arrived at the five star White Swan Hotel and settled in. The White Swan Hotel is affectionately called the White Stork Hotel because of the many adoptive families who stay there. It is located right down the street from the U.S. Consulate, so it's a convenient place to stay while taking care of the adoption paperwork. During our meals in the hotel, we watched with curiosity, longing, and a little fear as tables full of new parents tried to wrestle their new babies in their laps. Some babies wouldn't eat, some were sick and sleepy, while others devoured spoonfuls of rice congee as fast as their parents could feed them. It was a chilling and exciting reminder that our turn was coming next.

Our goal for the next two days in China was to stay healthy and rest. The weather was extremely hot and humid, and the air polluted. Jeff has serious allergies, and we both wanted to avoid terrible respiratory infections like the ones we had developed on our previous trip to China. It was important for us to maintain our strength and be in top condition for the adventure ahead. Since we had visited China before, we didn't feel obligated to do any touring. We visited some shops located within walking distance of the hotel. We found stores that stock their shelves with items they know adoptive families might want and need during their stay. Formula, diapers, medicines and snacks are also left behind by families who didn't need them and are available for free to future parents. The shops are brimming with beautiful Chinese silk dresses and pajamas, shoes that squeak when the child walks, Chinese cultural items, and souvenirs.

"Jeff, let's find gifts to give Adelynn on the anniversary of our adoption day," I suggested as we milled through the silk dresses.

We collected eighteen unique gifts so that she'd have a treasure from China to open every year on the anniversary of her adoption day. From Chinese toys for her to play with while she's still young to a pearl necklace and earrings to open when she turns eighteen. Jeff and I picked out some beautiful red silk fabric. I imagined us making (or having made) a lovely prom dress or a pantsuit for a special occasion. It was important for us to bring back as many mementos of her birth country as possible.

Forever Family

To understand your parents' love you must raise children yourself.

—Chinese proverb

After a few days rest in Guangzhou, it was time to fly to the province where our daughter resided. Our daughter was at the Jian City Welfare Institute, north of the city of Nanchang. Before we left for the airport, we walked to an Internet café down the street to send an email report home to family and friends. I wrote a quick summary of our trip thus far and sent it to over fifty people.

As I checked my email, I noticed a message from my friend Charlene. She traveled to China a few days earlier and had arrived in Nanchang that morning. I was anxious to read her report home to friends. She was traveling with her best friend, Shirley, because her husband was home with their older daughter, Lauren. Charlene's email mentioned what fun she and Shirley were having shopping their way through China. At the very end of the email it read, "We initially thought the babies were arriving tomorrow, but we've been told they'll be here today."

"Today?" I yelled out loud in disbelief.

Jeff raced over to the computer. We checked the date her email was sent. It was the same day. According to her note, the babies were arriving that very day. We looked at each other in panic. Jeff and I would be the last family to arrive in Nanchang. What if our daughter was already waiting for us at the hotel? I began to tremble.

Anxiously, we flew from Guangzhou to Nanchang, located in the Jiangxi province of China. We checked into the hotel in Nanchang and spoke briefly on the phone to our tour guide and translator, Angela. Charlene's email was correct. Two of the five families had already received their girls. Little Annie had already joined Steve and Cheryl, and Isabella was safely in Charlene's arms. The other three girls were expected within the hour.

We scurried around our room trying to unpack our mammoth bags and locate baby essentials. I was trembling, sick to my stomach, and sweating profusely because I felt so unprepared. Our master plan was dependent on our daughter arriving the NEXT day. We had hoped for an evening to unpack and get organized. I had planned for this moment for more than a year, yet it took me completely by surprise. We got as much unpacked and ready as we could, and within 45 minutes of arriving our phone rang.

"Hello, this is Angela," our translator said in her soft Chinese accent. "Come to my room and meet your daughter."

We dashed next door to Charlene's room.

"Charlene, she's here! She's here!" I squealed, leaping around the room like a little kid.

Charlene put her arm around me and gave me a warm, reassuring hug.

"Let's go meet your baby girl," she said lovingly with a smile.

Charlene grabbed our video camera, and Cheryl offered to take pictures. We hurried to Angela's room. The door was already open. I peeked in and saw three little girls being held by their beautiful Chinese caretakers. We walked in.

"Can you tell which little girl is ours?" I whispered to Jeff.

Jeff shrugged his shoulders. The referral photos of Ji Chen Ge were taken several months earlier when she was only a few months old, so it was impossible to tell. Angela spoke something in Chinese to one of the nannies, and she walked over to us holding a frightened little girl.

"Ji Chen Ge?" Angela asked.

"Yes!" we said in unison.

I looked at this little girl and couldn't believe we were finally meeting our daughter. She was so beautiful and small. She had dark hair with little curls and thin, tan legs. Her eyes were sad. The red welt visible in her referral picture was completely gone. The back of her head was covered with sores. She wore a white t-shirt, diaper, and tattered sandals. Her shoes caught my eye. They were plastic sandals with a worn Hello Kitty emblem barely attached to the top. For a child not yet walking, they seemed to have traveled many miles.

The nanny placed Ji Chen Ge in my arms.

"Hi," I whispered as I gently rubbed her back.

She was so light and petite, I was afraid I might drop her. I nervously smiled as the camera flashed. Jeff and I were in love. Very quiet, and scared, Ji Chen Ge stared at the TV blaring a Chinese movie. She didn't scream when she saw us, but secretly I wished she was as happy to see us as we were to see her. We just held her and gazed at her. This was our little girl.

"This is your daddy," I quietly said, as I lifted our daughter into Jeff's arms.

"Hello, my baby girl," Jeff said as he blinked back the tears.

Angela asked us if we had any questions for the nanny or the orphanage director. I had prepared a list of questions but couldn't remember anything to ask. I was overwhelmed and speechless. Fortunately, the orphanage director and nannies were staying overnight in the hotel, and we could meet with them the following day for questions.

"Okay," Angela said, as if to say we were finished.

"Okay what?" I asked in confusion.

"You can take your daughter back to your room," she said with a smile.

I must have had a terrified look on my face, but her smile seemed to say "Don't worry, you'll be fine."

Once alone in our room, the reality set in for both of us. Jeff was instantly in love and overwhelmed with more emotion than he was used to feeling all at once.

"She's just beautiful," Jeff said with the cracking voice of a man stuffing back tears.

Adelynn sat in his lap and seemed to be exhausted.

I was anxious about the logistics of taking care of her. I didn't have much experience caring for a baby. I nervously ran around the room making preparations. As I changed her diaper, I noticed her bottom was dry and clean without any signs of diaper rash. I tried to find a sleeper for her to change into. We quickly discovered she was much smaller than the referral report stated. Nothing we brought would fit her. Having been warned that the babies had never been in air conditioning before, it was important she sleep in something warmer than her flimsy t-shirt. I went next door and borrowed a sleeper from our trusted friend, Charlene.

I had never dressed a child in a one-piece sleeper before. I slipped Adelynn's arms through the sleeves and tried to insert her feet. I stretched and pulled the material to slide in her feet, but they didn't fit. Adelynn lay sadly limp as I struggled to dress her. I finally realized I was doing something wrong, so I started again. I tried putting her in the sleeper feet first this time. Her arms easily slid into the sleeves, and I zipped her up.

I felt foolish that I didn't even know how to put her pajamas on correctly. My feelings of inadequacy mounted at the thought of the many more mistakes I would make in her lifetime. I gave her a hug and told her I still had lots to learn. Her eyes looked away. She was emotionally detached. Those dark eyes spoke volumes. The poor thing was taken from the only home she had known, had made a very long journey, and was handed over to strangers who looked different from anyone she had ever seen before, and spoke an entirely different language. Our union was bittersweet.

I rushed to prepare a bottle. Normally the orphanage provides families with some of the formula they used for the baby, but the orphanage director hadn't brought any. That meant we would be giving her the formula we had brought. I knew from my research this would be a bad start. Switching formula is rough on a baby under normal circumstances. I worried this would cause her body added stress. Many of the babies in the orphanages are fed thick rice cereal in their bottles and drink it very hot. I knew enough to prepare it this way. We widened the nipple to make it easier for her to drink from. We gave her the bottle, and she sucked it breathlessly.

"She must be really hungry," Jeff guessed as we watched her.

"Is she able to get anything out of it?" I questioned noticing the milk wasn't emptying from the bottle.

The nipple opening still wasn't wide enough for her. Our obvious language barrier was a problem, so I created hand signs for things.[15] For the bottle, I made a sucking sound while putting my thumb towards my mouth. While Jeff tried to widen the opening of the nipple some more, Adelynn started repeating the sucking sound I had been making as if to say, "Bring on that bottle." We were amazed at how quickly she caught on to the sign, and we were pleased she was able to communicate her wishes. We ruined two nipples before we finally made the opening the right size. She gulped down the bottle and fell fast asleep. We gently placed her in the crib, then sat and watched her. She was so beautiful, sweet, and innocent. She was a survivor. Adelynn Chen-Ge Woodard was finally with her forever momma and daddy.

Adelynn didn't sleep very well and cried out many times in her sleep. Every time she stirred or moved, I immediately bolted awake. She had only four top teeth and four bottom teeth, but I could hear her grinding them during her sleep. I slept very little and felt as if I needed to be guarding her during the night. She awoke early and was sadly lethargic. Her nose was running profusely, and the discharge looked infected. She needed a warm bath, so we let her watch in the bathroom mirror as we gave her a quick wash in the sink. The orphanages do not bathe the babies, but wipe them down with a washcloth. Her first bath was as traumatic as we anticipated. She was fascinated with the running water, but her hair had never been wet. She was terrified. She shook in hysteria as we quickly washed the soap from her hair.

We snuggled her in a big fluffy towel and rubbed lotion on her dry, irritated skin. She watched us intently in the mirror as we gave her a little massage and cuddled her in our arms. We could tell by the look on her face this attachment technique was working. Our hugs seemed foreign to her, but it was obviously something she craved.

We gathered all our documents and prepared for our day of paperwork with the Chinese officials. All five families and babies were loaded into a van and taken to the Civil Affairs Office to complete the Chinese government portion of our adoption. Adelynn lay on my chest, falling in and out of sleep. She didn't seem well. Our body heat was stifling and we were both drenched in sweat. It was impossible to tell if she had a fever because we were both so overheated. We waited in a hot, crowded room and tried to calm our nervous new daughters. There were many critical documents to bring and complete, and one thing out of order would put a halt to the entire process. The Chinese government is unforgiving about mistakes or misplaced paperwork. Our fingerprints and Adelynn's footprints were taken in red sticky ink and pressed onto important Chinese documents which we couldn't read. We shuffled from room to room for pictures, interviews, and payments to officials. I glanced over at the other families and saw the tension on their faces. They were just as overwhelmed as we were. It was a stressful experience, as we never knew what was coming up next or what paperwork was needed when.

"Raise your right hand," Angela instructed us. She translated for the official.

"Do you promise to always care for this girl? To give her a proper education and safe home? And to never abandon her?"

My throat felt choked hearing the "abandon" word.

"Yes, we promise," Jeff and I replied with our hands held high. Jeff was holding Adelynn with his other hand and her head plopped on his shoulder as if she knew she could now relax.

Our adoption was official. We were now a family. We affectionately call this day our "Forever Family Day."

After the chaotic paperwork, we visited a department store to purchase supplies. The shopping was difficult since there were five families and only one translator. Our guide, Angela, did her best to run from person to person to read labels and translate the wording on containers.

Even though we had Adelynn for only a short time, we knew something wasn't right. She looked sickly and felt feverish. In the outdoor heat, her perspiration was irritating the sores on her head. I worried the sores might be scabies. They looked like bedsores, but we couldn't tell. She scratched at them with her fingernails making the wounds even worse. Jeff took her into the air-conditioned minivan while I gathered some essentials. While waiting in the van, many Chinese people stopped to stare. They pressed their faces against the glass to get a better look at Jeff and Adelynn. When they saw Jeff sitting in the van with Adelynn they would give the thumbs-up sign and smile because they knew Adelynn would be going to a good home. They were pleased. I purchased some Chinese formula, rice cereal, bottled water, and about a dozen Ramen-like noodles in Styrofoam cups. These cups of noodles would provide us many hot and easy lunches in our hotel room.

By the time we made it back to the hotel, Adelynn's health seemed to decline. Deciding she needed professional care, we visited the hotel clinic. It was nicer than I imagined it would be but still way below our country's standard of sterile conditions. A woman with a badge that read "Doctor" welcomed us into the small room. We tried to communicate with her, but she didn't speak a word of English. I found it strange she didn't know any English. Higher education in China includes extensive study in the English language. We called Angela and asked her to translate for us. The "Doctor" only glanced at Adelynn before pulling out medicine. She didn't look in Adelynn's ears, feel her glands, or do any of the typical screenings a doctor in the U.S. would do in an exam. Adelynn had protruding swollen glands, green discharge in her eye, open sores on the back of her head, and thick drainage from her nose, none of which the "Doctor" noticed until I showed her with Angela's help. She might have been a nurse or nurse's aide but almost certainly not a doctor. Nonetheless, she prescribed an antibiotic cream for the sores and a three-day supply of oral antibiotic for the rest of Adelynn's symptoms. Even I knew a mere three-day supply of antibiotics wouldn't be enough to clear up the infection, but it was a start. At least this would back down the infection obviously raging inside her until we could obtain more medicine at the White Swan Hotel in Guangzhou.

In the evening, we were invited back to Angela's room to meet the orphanage director for questions. Adelynn became very upset when we walked into the room. She looked away from the orphanage director and nanny and tucked her head in Jeff's neck. It was as if she were afraid she was being sent back. I felt myself tearing up at Adelynn's distress when we saw them, but I could tell by something in their eyes that the orphanage director and nanny truly cared for Adelynn. We didn't know if the nanny who handed Adelynn to us was just someone who helped deliver her to the hotel or if she had been a significant caregiver to Adelynn. Regardless, they both appeared to be happy about Adelynn's new family.

The orphanage had received the disposable camera and questions we had mailed to them. The orphanage director brought my sheet of questions with him and had filled out every line. They took pictures of Adelynn's life at the orphanage with the disposable camera and even had the pictures developed so we were able to immediately see where Adelynn had lived.

The pictures were difficult for us to view. The orphanage building was stark white, made of cinderblocks, and had an institutional look. There were no decorations or anything resembling a nursery or place where children would play. There were pictures of Adelynn and other babies outside, confined in little bamboo chairs. I already knew that many orphanages keep older infants in walkers or chairs like these during the day, but I was shocked to see Adelynn screaming and struggling in her chair. The look on her face sickened me. Some of the babies had white salve on their faces and heads, probably to treat the heat rash inevitable in the indescribable heat of the south China summer. While I knew that orphanages like hers were often understaffed, operating on meager funds, and understood that they did their best with what they had, the conditions I saw in these photos were deplorable by our standards.

The pictures made me ill. I felt a deep pain inside me, an ache I can't describe. My hands trembled. I gasped in tears. I'm usually a very emotionally balanced person, but an earthquake of emotion was building in me I'd never experienced. The thought of my baby spending an entire year in those conditions without a family was more than I could stand. While they were difficult to view, we were grateful for the pictures and the glimpse into Adelynn's first year of life. All I could do was weep and thank them.

Back in our room, Adelynn and Jeff were able to relax and fall asleep for the night. I tossed around trying to settle my thoughts but was unsuccessful. I got out of bed and went into the bathroom where I could turn on the light without disturbing them. I sat on the edge of the bathtub and quietly cried into one of the hotel bath towels. I released every positive and negative feeling stuffed inside me. I sobbed out of exhaustion, frustration and fear. I let the impact of our adoption experience come to the surface. We became instant parents to an almost one-year old child. She counted on us to do what was best for her. I was happy to have Adelynn in our life, but I was scared. Raising her would be one of the most important and crucial things I would do in my lifetime. The responsibility was staggering. I cried for almost half an hour until I felt better. I washed my face with cold water and went back to bed.

Adelynn awoke the next morning screaming in pain. Switching formulas was brutal on her. She struggled for almost an hour to have a bowel movement. We felt helpless. She lay on top of a pillow, crying and straining. It angered me that she was experiencing this unnecessarily because we didn't have the orphanage formula she was familiar with when we first received her. If only the orphanage staff had remembered to bring some formula. After it passed, she fell asleep from fatigue. We sat on the bed and watched her sleep. Her little head was covered in perspiration and her sores were greasy from the medicine. Her hair looked dry and unhealthy, yet continued to flip and curl in every direction. She was tattered, but beautiful.

Fortunately, after her rest she seemed much better. The antibiotics had begun to work their magic, and her condition was improving. At breakfast she happily sampled banana bread, scrambled eggs and anything bite sized she could pick up. She wiggled in our laps which made it difficult for us to eat. She grabbed at spoons and napkins, and nearly dumped over my orange juice. A sympathetic waiter wheeled over a high chair for us to use. Adelynn shrieked in terror when we tried to put her in it and shook violently. She reacted like a wild animal struggling for survival. She yanked her hair and clawed at her face. This reaction continued for many weeks when we placed her in any kind of seat. The pictures brought to us by the orphanage director provided a clue to her behavior. Whether she was afraid she would be "locked" in it, or afraid she'd be left there, we didn't push the issue and kept her on my lap. She was expressing her feelings and learning we would respond to her needs.

After breakfast, we loaded ourselves into the minivan with the rest of our group. We visited a beautiful temple. A giant gold Buddha was seated on a raised platform. Sticks of incense burned at his feet as worshippers bowed. A group of women were intrigued when they saw Jeff holding Adelynn. They spoke some broken English.

"Hello, you baby?" a woman asked pointing to Adelynn.

"Yes, she's my daughter," Jeff proudly replied.

"She looked like you," another chimed in. "Are you minxst?"

"Minxst?" Jeff asked and looked at me. I shrugged my shoulders. Jeff finally figured it out.

"Mixed? Oh, am I mixed?" They all nodded thinking Jeff looked part Chinese.

"No, I'm not Chinese," Jeff answered, "I'm part American Indian."

They looked at each other in confusion. I'm sure they were thinking of Americans, Indians from India, and trying to fit the two together.

Wanting to play with Adelynn, they tried to grab her from Jeff's arms. Adelynn gave them a very angry look and swatted a hand their way. She made it clear she wasn't leaving her daddy.

We stopped at a porcelain factory. The Jiangxi province is known for its production of exquisite porcelain, so it seemed fitting that we bring back a memento. We bought a gorgeous tea serving set decorated in traditional Chinese design. It was packed in an elegant silk covered box and could easily be stuffed into one of our suitcases.

We stayed the next few days in Nanchang, until Adelynn's Chinese passport and adoption papers were translated and notarized. We spent a lot of our time in our hotel room. The other families were eager shoppers. Little Isabella rode in a carrier snuggled close to Charlene's chest and seemed perfectly happy as Charlene haggled for bargains in the local shops. Like mother, like daughter. In our previous trips to China, we had done our fair share of shopping. Adelynn was still uncomfortable with the group and wanted nothing to do with shopping. She seemed to enjoy the time alone with us in our room as it was quiet, and the cool temperature was a welcome break from the extreme heat. She smiled, laughed, and busily played with stacking cups for hours. She showed no signs of developmental delays at all and could walk with assistance. She quickly caught on to silly games. She said "ah-oh" when she'd drop something and would put her hands on her head as if to say, "Where did it go?" Adelynn loved to be playfully tossed around by daddy.

"Da-da, da-da, da-da," she chanted over and over again as Jeff swung her in his arms. She trusted him, and was showing signs of a promising gymnast.

I brought a small book of family pictures for Adelynn to look at. It included grandparents, Adelynn's referral picture, our dogs, and us. We would point to the picture of our dog, Andrew, and say, "Ah, Andrew, pet Andrew nice." We had a book called "Pat the Puppy" so that she could feel the softness of the puppy's fur and get the idea of what the dogs would feel like. Children in orphanages often have never seen animals, so it was important for us to prepare her for our three big dogs waiting at home. She seemed very receptive to the pictures. I prayed she'd be happy to meet them.

Before we left for China, I taped over an hour of our dogs barking. There were always opportunities to record our dogs in a fit of barking. Both the mailman and Jeff's arrival home from work would always send them into barking madness. We brought the tape and a small cassette player with us and played the dog barking sounds in our hotel room. The idea was to get Adelynn used to the noises our dogs made so that it wouldn't terrify her when we got home. We played the dog barking tape at a soft level, increasing the volume a little more each day. It frightened her a little at first, but she eventually adjusted well to it.

"Adelynn, see the doggies," I pointed to the picture of our dogs. "Hear the doggies go woof-woof."

"Is this dog barking thing really gonna prepare her for our dogs?" Jeff questioned. "The other hotel guests must think we're housing a dozen dogs in here!"

Within a few short days she was comfortable with the rambunctious barking and howling of our four-legged family members. My plan was working.

Adelynn continued to sleep restlessly but could settle back down if we rubbed her tummy. Despite her lack of sleep, she woke up refreshed, alert, and ready to play. The day-to-day improvements in her health were remarkable. Love, food and proper medicine were working miracles. We watched our daughter bloom right before our very eyes!

She listened energetically to a tape of Chinese music we purchased in a local shop. She acted as if she had never been exposed to music, but she clearly understood some of what was being said on the tape. Our guide, Angela, spoke to Adelynn in Chinese, and Adelynn responded to most everything she said. Angela told Adelynn her doll was hungry, and Adelynn placed a Cheerio on the doll's mouth. She was less than a year old at the time and understood everything said to her in Chinese. She was very aware of what was going on.

We gave her a bath again, and this time she was less fearful. She stood in the sink as we washed her little body. Still, her body showed signs of her former life, as there were many bug bites on her legs and her skin was very dry. She kicked her legs in the water, and we got soaking wet.

"Hey," I joked. "Quit that!" She thought that was funny and continued to splash.

She was small and thin, but very strong. Adelynn's clothing selection was slim to none since all the clothes we brought with us were too large. Her diapers were two sizes too big and went almost up to her chin. Her referral information stated that at ten months old she was 17 pounds, but she was actually only 15 pounds when we got her at almost 12 months old. She was the tiniest of all the little girls in our group. We tried shopping for clothes that would fit, but the selection was poor where we were located and she was fearful in crowds. We borrowed clothing from other families and sent clothing to be cleaned by the hotel every day.

On our fifth day in Nanchang, Adelynn's Chinese passport and adoption documents were ready, marking the last stage of our five-day paperwork process in Nanchang. We were permitted to leave the province and fly to Guangzhou for the visa paperwork with the American Consulate. That evening the families enjoyed a celebratory dinner together downstairs in the hotel. Adelynn ravenously consumed carrots, potatoes, bananas, and stew meat. Enthusiastically, she finished her meal and walked out of the restaurant holding daddy's hands. Adelynn's confidence continued to blossom every day.

After dinner we decided to investigate the hotel playroom. The girls were still full of energy and some playtime sounded like a good idea. It was a nice playroom, just the right size for our girls, with little slides, rockers, balls, and chutes to crawl through. Adelynn and Isabella, Charlene's little girl, toddled around the room with our assistance. I looked forward to our daughters growing up together and enjoyed watching them interact. The girls played with balls, rode rocking horses and slid down slides until they collapsed in fatigue.

Once Jeff and Adelynn were asleep, I slipped out to the hotel business center to send a quick email home. Below is the email I sent five days after Adelynn was placed in our arms.

July 6, 2001

Hello all,

What a wild couple of days! Jeff and Adelynn are asleep in our room so I have a few minutes to write. Adelynn has continued to blossom more and more every day. She is a wild woman! She's very active, quick and determined. She's very strong and just gets stronger every day. She mimics us and we've developed these silly games between us. Jeff has become the human amusement park. She loves to be tossed around and climbs him like a jungle gym. We blow on her belly (we call them raspberries) and she tries to do it back to us. Yesterday she gave Jeff a raspberry and he let out a little yelp. She did it so hard that it made a hicky on his belly. I found it hysterical! Better not laugh too much because I'm sure I'll get my turn.

The first day we had her she could walk with assistance in a stagger kind of way. This morning, she started walking with only one hand for assistance. She'll be on her own within a week or two…maybe even walk off the plane by herself. Yikes!

This is definitely a crash course in parenting. We've certainly learned a lot about caring for a baby in the past five days. Here is my top ten list of lessons learned the hard way. (Drum roll please)

10. Do not change a baby's diaper while they are asleep and expect them to remain asleep.

9. Administer purple medicine BEFORE dressing baby in white jumper.

8. Do not toss a baby in the air above your head after feeding them rice cereal.

7. Always check that both socks are still on baby before leaving restaurant.

6. If baby has eight teeth, insert cheerio into their mouth and retrieve fingers QUICKLY.

5. Both dogs and babies put disgusting things in their mouth and won't let go of them easily.

4. Mashed bananas are very sticky in your hair.

3. If baby's nose explodes with undesirable secretions, wipe it quickly or they will eat it.

2. Packets of sugar, empty water bottles and paper placemats are more exciting at the dinner table than a musical Elmo rattle.

1. There's nothing more heart warming than a toothy grin from a baby that adores you!

Better get back to the room before the little tornado awakens. Thank you all for your emails. I haven't had time to reply but please know I have received them and appreciate hearing from you. More later…

Love,

The Woodard's

The next day, we packed up our disastrous room and prepared to leave for Guangzhou. On the ride to the airport, we noticed huge fields of rice paddies and asked the driver to stop to let us take some pictures. The rice fields looked like little sprigs of grass in a murky pool of water. They were budding and ready for harvest. It was like a view you'd see in National Geographic Magazine with the city of Nanchang in the background.

Our minds were filled with mixed emotion as we left this province where our daughter had lived. We watched an old man who looked at least 80 years old pedal a dilapidated bicycle hauling heavy sacks of rice. What would Adelynn's life have been like if she stayed in China? Would she someday be stooped in these rice fields in the hot scorching sun? We teared up as we drove away and felt blessed to be bringing Adelynn home to America where her choices would be many.

Paperwork Completion

The beginning and the end reach out their hands to each other.

——Chinese proverb

A terrible hurricane was blowing towards Hong Kong and was scheduled to hit the day we were to fly to Guangzhou. Hong Kong is just a short ferry ride southeast of Guangzhou, so we were in its path. We nervously boarded our flight from Nanchang to Guangzhou and prayed for a safe trip.

During the flight, the movie screen aired Tom & Jerry cartoons. The Chinese passengers wholeheartedly laughed out loud at each bang and fall of the cat and mouse.

"Am I missing something?" I quietly asked Jeff. "I've watched Tom & Jerry lots of times but have never laughed out loud at them."

"They're just cracking up, aren't they?" Jeff and I couldn't help but laugh. I noticed other Americans on the plane looking around with smiles, as if they also found it strange the Chinese passengers would find this cartoon so amusing.

Adelynn's ear infection was still a concern, so we fed her graham crackers during the take-off and landing, hoping the chewing would reduce the pressure in her ears. We experienced a little turbulence on the descent but nothing serious. Adelynn fared very well on her first airplane ride.

We were all extremely relieved to arrive at the lovely White Swan Hotel. We were one step closer to home. The families met for dinner at Lucy's

American Cafe near the hotel and enjoyed some American-style food. We were all happy to forego another meal of rice. Little Annie, Isabella and Adelynn adapted very well to the new menu. They nibbled bites of french fries, cheeseburgers, and raviolis from all of our plates. Even though I rarely eat burgers, I had been craving a burger, fries, and Coke. We were reinforcing the American stereotype of junk food eaters and enjoying every last bite.

Late that evening with Adelynn fast asleep, Jeff watched Chinese television while I wrote in my journal. We could hear that Annie wasn't ready for bed. Her daddy, Steve, walked her up and down the hallway of the hotel as she babbled and chattered. Poor Steve was exhausted and needed rest, but Annie was enjoying her walk.

"There goes Annie," we joked hearing her little voice pass by our door. "Still going." Ten minutes would pass and we'd hear her again. "And going." We fell asleep before Annie did.

In the morning, we walked across the street from the hotel to have Adelynn's picture taken for her medical examination. The hurricane had settled into a storm, so we walked quickly in the rain. The picture for her medical exam was the equivalent of getting a passport photo. The room was hot and humid from the rain, and dozens of families with babies were squeezed into a very small room. We had to sit Adelynn on an elevated chair for her picture. She sat there for less than sixty seconds, but it was enough to upset her for the next half hour. Anytime we sat her down on something she panicked. After her very unhappy photo, we walked a few blocks to get her medical examination.

It was total chaos. More than one hundred people were crammed into a building the size of a convenience store. We were pushed from one room to another for each separate exam. Adelynn had her hearing and vision tested, along with a quick physical. She screamed at every exam. We were pushed from one area to the next, paperwork stamped and then pushed into another room. Just as soon as our exam was complete, we left the building. We were so hot and miserable. We went immediately back to the hotel to cool off in the air conditioning and take a nap.

When we awoke, I peeked outside our hotel window to see if the rain had stopped. I was shocked to see the main entrances of our hotel flooded with rushing water on two sides. The White Swan Hotel is situated on the Shamian Island, overlooking the Pearl River. The hurricane caused the river to swell and flood the streets surrounding it.

"If I have to be stranded somewhere, it might as well be in a five star hotel," I teased, observing the situation down below. Despite the rising water, people continued to walk through the murky sludge and go on about their daily business.

"Hey, isn't that Cheryl?" Jeff spotted her and the group wading through the water with packages in their hands.

"I can't believe it! There's a flood and they're STILL shopping!" We couldn't help but laugh at our friends' determination to hunt down bargains. These people were born to shop. By evening the waters had receded, and shopkeepers were airing out their stores. One shop owner said this was the highest the water had risen in over 40 years.

One member from each of the five families went to Angela's room to review our final paperwork in preparation for the United States Consulate appointment. She walked us step-by-step through the complicated documents and checked them for accuracy. Our appointment with the U.S. Consulate would be in two days and our paperwork needed to be in perfect order. After the checking and double-checking, I felt at ease that we were properly prepared.

Adelynn went to sleep without much problem but woke up at one a.m. very upset. She was hysterical, and nothing we did seemed to help. She screamed a blood-curdling cry and thrashed about for two solid hours. We felt bad that the hotel guests on our floor didn't get much of a good night's sleep, but there was nothing we could do to calm her. We had read about babies experiencing a grieving process that can occur days, or even weeks, after they're placed with their new families. I knew there was nothing else

I could do but offer her my love. I held her and tears dripped down my cheeks as she cried to the point of breathless exhaustion.

Adelynn awoke the next morning feeling much better, but she continued to cling to Jeff most of the day. She felt great comfort and security with him. Many of the babies bond first to the mothers and then to their daddies later. Adelynn formed an instant bond with Jeff and only later warmed up to me. When I met the orphanage director, I got a distinct feeling he cared for Adelynn. I suspect he had spent time with the children, so they were used to being around a man. Jeff has some American Indian heritage, so his dark almond eyes and dark hair might have looked familiar and comforting. With my red hair, green eyes and six-foot tall stature, I'm sure I was a scary sight. It's understandable her first instinct was to go to Jeff. It was disappointing to not be the favorite, but I could handle it better than Jeff would have. He was crazy in love with our little girl and never wanted to put her down. I jokingly called him a "baby hog" since Adelynn's feet never seemed to touch the ground.

Before our meeting at the American Consulate, I reviewed our paperwork one last time to make sure we were ready. The American Consulate building is located less than a block from the hotel. Our group of families walked nervously together. There were guards outside the Consulate building and a very long line of Chinese people. The Chinese spend days waiting in line in hopes of obtaining a visa to enter the United States. As Americans, we walked right up to the front of the line and were ushered in. I felt both proud and embarrassed to be treated so special. We are Americans simply by virtue of where we are born. We don't even realize how lucky we are. These Chinese people were prepared to make insurmountable sacrifices to visit our country, and we take the honor for granted. I hoped Adelynn would someday understand the blessing of freedom.

Our paperwork was checked again before we entered the meeting with our consulate officer. One member of the family meets with the officer, so we decided since I had completed all the paperwork, I would be best prepared for the meeting.

"Woodard," the officer called, holding a file folder under her arm. I walked up to the table. The consulate official was very nice and asked for certain documents. I quickly presented each one, but froze when she asked for Adelynn's visa photos.

"Visa photos?" I asked in confusion. Somehow I had missed that we were supposed to bring them. I panicked. A surge of heat rushed up my neck and face as I dug through my bag. I had no idea what I had done with them. I looked back at Jeff and saw the anxiety building in his face.

"It's okay, take your time," the officer reassured me. I continued to flip through my papers, trying not to overreact. The paperwork process is very detailed, and one mistake could be devastating. Completely by luck, the visa photos were pressed against the inside of my folder. I triumphantly pulled them out, "I have them!" I shouted. I turned to Jeff and saw his chest rise and relax with a sigh of relief. Our officer smiled, and the rest of the process went smoothly. Documents were signed, stamped, and everything was finalized. The next day we could pick up Adelynn's visa and head home.

The families celebrated our paperwork completion with a grand night at the Hard Rock Café. There was an Asian band playing American music at a festive volume. The food was excellent, and we were all ravenous for American cuisine. We bought Hard Rock Café Guangzhou T-shirts as souvenirs for friends back home and even purchased Adelynn a "My first Hard Rock Café Guangzhou T-shirt." Adelynn developed a love for french fries. She held the salty fry in her tiny fingers, feeling very pleased with herself as she nibbled it. The men all took their new daughters on the dance floor for their first "daddy-daughter dance." I watched as Jeff swayed back and forth with Adelynn in his arms. My eyes filled with tears to see these men love their little girls so deeply. These girls were already loved beyond words and their lives with us were just beginning.

At breakfast the next morning all the families met for group pictures. There is a red couch in the White Swan Hotel that has become a traditional location for group photos. We took pictures of just the girls on the couch together, mothers with babies, fathers with babies, and all of us together, including our guide, Angela. We had all shared an incredible experience that would bond us for life. I intended to keep in touch with the families and looked forward to watching the girls grow up to be young women.

In the afternoon we walked back to the American Consulate to pick up Adelynn's visa. We now had everything we needed to take Adelynn home. I finally felt able to relax a bit. The stress of worrying that the paperwork might somehow be incorrect was over. We happily packed our bags for the trip home. Adelynn was our daughter both emotionally and legally. Nothing would ever change that.

That night, Angela took our group to a Chinese restaurant for our final meal together. It was a peaceful place with a long walkway leading over a water garden with beautifully hung lanterns. Along the path, the evening's "entrées" were caged for selection. Everything including snake, duck, rabbits, fish, and anything in between was available for consumption. The cages were quite dirty and smelled of feces. The sights and smells ruined our appetites.

"Do they bathe the animals before they cook them?" Jeff joked watching me cringe at the smell.

I had a strong urge to free all the animals but knew my efforts would be futile.

At the meal, our server introduced different dishes by placing them on a large lazy suzan located in the center of our table. The rotating lazy suzan makes it easy for the guests to reach each dish. The custom is to use your chopsticks to grab the food from the dish and put it on your plate. Throughout the meal you use your chopsticks to take seconds. Many tourists are often uncomfortable with dirty chopsticks in the communal dishes. Angela would explain the basic ingredients of each dish, but everyone was a little squeamish about the meat. Charlene and I exchanged knowing glances. We had made it this far without developing any stomach problems and didn't want to eat something that might disagree with us, making our journey home miserable. We were gracious and appreciative of her thoughtfulness, but we all left hungry.

"Angela was so sweet to bring us here," I commented to Jeff, "but I couldn't eat the meat. I'm starving."

"I'm still hungry, too," Jeff agreed. "Let's order some food to our hotel room. We can order from that American restaurant that delivers, Danny's Bagel."[16]

Jeff and I played it safe and ordered raviolis and french fries to our room that night.

Going Home

○ ○

Wheresoever you go, go with all your heart.

——*Confucius*

Many international airlines require you to reconfirm before you leave for your return flight. The reservation may not be considered actually booked until you reconfirm and get a seat assigned. We had run into problems with this on past international trips and knew to take care of this issue days before our flight home. We reconfirmed with China Southern Airlines and even received a reconfirmation number stamped on our tickets. What we didn't realize, however, was that we needed to reconfirm our seats, as well. We were reserved on the flight but without seat assignments.

Once at the airport, the airline desk assigned our seats. Since it was the last minute, they were located in totally different ends of business class. When we got onboard, I thought we could surely find some people to switch seats with us, but the entire business class was filled with adoptive families and their babies all taking advantage of the special adoptive family fare. Over thirty babies and their parents filled every seat and wouldn't be moved, or they would be separated like us. I think the fatigue must have gotten to me because I started crying. I knew Adelynn would want to sleep with Jeff, and I didn't want to be separated from them for this long journey home.

"Please," I begged the airline steward, "our family can't be split up!"

The steward was sympathetic and tried to find someone who would trade with us, but it was useless. Finally, a nice lady sitting in the seat directly in front of me offered to trade seats with Jeff. It was better than one of us handling Adelynn solo, so we gratefully accepted. Adelynn preferred to spend most of the flight in Jeff's arms. I handed him the essentials from behind. She pulled out the magazines from the seat in front of him and tried to climb over the top of the seat. She was incredibly active for two hours and then collapsed asleep in Jeff's arms. Jeff was unable to put his tray table down to eat with her asleep on top of him, so I had to feed him dinner one spoonful at a time over the top of the seat.

"Here comes the train," I joked. "Choo-choo!" I chugged the spoon of beef tips and rice towards his mouth.

"Funny," Jeff whispered trying not to awaken Adelynn. "Just don't spill it on me."

It was too bad we couldn't have been seated next to each other. It would have been so much easier. With over 30 babies on the flight, there wasn't a moment when one of them wasn't crying. It was a long 15 hours.

When we touched down in Los Angeles, the passengers in business class clapped and cheered. Under the new American citizenship law, our newly adopted Chinese girls instantly became citizens once we landed on American soil. Adelynn was officially ours and now a United States citizen. We collected our bags and submitted Adelynn's paperwork to Immigration for admittance into the U.S. Her documents were processed, passport stamped, and we were free to go.

We checked into a hotel in Los Angeles to stay the night and rest. We knew it would be too exhausting to continue to Tulsa after our long flight from China. Once in our room, we ordered a barbecue chicken pizza, salads, and ice cold Coke. We ravenously ate it, and to this day I think it was the best meal I've ever tasted. No rice, just good old American fare. We fell asleep by midnight, but Adelynn was still on China time. She was wide-awake again at two a.m., tumbling on the bed, making pow-wow sounds with her mouth. If Adelynn was awake, there was no sleeping for us. She was adapting to hotel rooms and made herself comfortable. We monitored her with half-opened sleepy eyes. She slid off the bed and crawled into the bathroom. Before we knew it, she was unrolling the toilet paper and stuffing it in the toilet. We were exhausted, but sleep was no longer an option.

"She's not going back to sleep," Jeff moaned in exhaustion. And she wasn't.

"Well, let's order another pizza then. I'm starved." I was ready to eat again.

We ordered another tasty barbecue pizza with Coke at four a.m. and prepared for the last leg of our journey home.

We flew from Los Angeles to Dallas with Adelynn fast asleep in Jeff's lap. At least one of us was able to sleep. Once in Dallas, we found many American Airlines flights to Tulsa, but unfortunately most were on prop planes. I don't usually mind the small planes, but they are not air conditioned during boarding, and it was summer. Dallas heat speaks for itself. We boarded the plane and sat on the tarmac for almost an hour in sweltering heat.

"This is unbearable," I complained to Jeff. Adelynn's cheeks turned red.

By the time the plane took off we were all covered in sweat and wilted. The flight was less than an hour long, so the plane was just starting to cool off at landing. Adelynn handled the heat very well but was fussy and ready to get out.

As the plane descended into Tulsa, the flat fields of Oklahoma looked comforting. Of all our international trips, this homecoming was the most dramatic.

"Adelynn," I slid her on my lap so she could look out the window, "this is Oklahoma. Your home, honey! See the cows." The sight of those silly cows made my eyes fill up with tears.

The plane landed and I said a little thank you prayer under my breath. It felt good to be home. We walked down the jetway in nervous anticipation.

"Adelynn, get ready to meet your new family and friends," I whispered as we neared the end of the ramp. "They've all been waiting for you."

We were greeted by a group of more than fifty people cheering and clapping. Most of them had tears in their eyes. I was prepared for the welcoming, but unprepared for the surge of emotion I would feel. I was so happy to be home, and felt so loved and supported, I burst into tears. I eagerly hugged our friends and family. Passengers on our flight stopped to clap and congratulate us. We created quite a roadblock. My friend Dana, whose dossier was delayed in China, stood in front of the crowd with a teary smile.

"Oh, Sarah, she's beautiful," Dana whispered. The two of us exchanged a warm hug. She would leave two weeks later to bring home her daughter, Susanna.

Other adoptive families were there, too. Adelynn was greeted with many smiles from the older Chinese girls. Claire, the little girl from our church nursery, jumped up and down to greet us.

"Oh, Claire, you're here!" I picked her up, and gave her the biggest hug.

"Does she play Candyland?" Claire enthusiastically asked.

"Not yet," I laughed. I was so happy to see her. I felt like I might cry again as I held her. Jeff and I introduced Adelynn to her new family and friends. Many commented on how beautiful she was, and congratulated us on our new daughter. I worried that the crowd of people would scare or upset Adelynn, but she wasn't bothered by it at all.

"Adelynn, this is your Grandma, Grandpa, and Memaw," I said introducing her to the family. My mother and Jeff's mother were both bursting to hold her, but Adelynn was overwhelmed with the crowd and clutched Jeff for security. She offered a dimpled smile to each, and the grandmas melted. Adelynn's new cousin, Rachel, presented her with Winnie the Pooh and Eeyore stuffed animals. Adelynn was unsure about the animals, looked them over, and handed them back. They would eventually become favorite bedtime companions. When we introduced her to Aunt Brenda and Uncle Bill, she leaned over and gave her Uncle Bill a kiss on the nose.

We were shocked at how comfortable she was with her new family. It was as if she knew she was home.

Our Family's Adjustment

o o o o o o o o o o o o o o o o o o o o o o o o o o o o o o o

The road to greatness begins at home.

——Chinese proverb

O ur long, grueling journey home and jumping 15 time zones left us with a major case of jet lag. Adelynn was still on China time, and we were terribly fatigued from skipping two nights of sleep. Our muscles ached, our eyes stung, and my hands trembled for no apparent reason.

Adelynn did not sleep well at night. When she did sleep, she was restless. She'd scream continually throughout the night. We attributed it to the jet lag and the obvious adjustment she must have been going through. Excited well-meaning family and friends called us, anxious to hear of our trip and meet the newest addition to the family. We were touched by their enthusiasm, but they had no idea of the depth of our exhaustion. I would spend nearly an hour getting Adelynn to sleep for a nap when the phone would ring or someone would drop by. She'd awaken suddenly, and the quick ten minutes she was asleep made her irritable and unlikely to fall asleep again soon. Jeff and I were desperate for rest, but little did we know we were in for a very long road of constant fatigue.

Adelynn took to our dogs immediately, and our four legged children acted like she'd always been there. The first night home she said all three of their names. Andrew was affectionately called "Ba-boo," Jacob was "Ay-cup" and Marcie was "Mmmm." We talked about each of them extensively while in China, so she was familiar with them when she finally met them. She wrapped her arms around Andrew, our 110-pound lab, put her head on his bulging belly and gave him a big hug. She enjoyed calling their names and having them run to her. She occasionally whacked them with a toy or pulled too hard on an ear, but they didn't seem to mind. We were very relieved the whole family was getting along.

Adelynn enjoyed exploring her new home. She crawled with great speed from room to room. It didn't take long for us to discover what areas of the house were insufficiently childproofed.

Clothing Adelynn was still a problem even though we were home. The outfits we purchased before leaving on our trip were all too big for her, so she was still wearing the few things we pieced together in China. I was overwhelmed with our transition and not having enough clean clothes caused me great anxiety.

"Adelynn has been wearing the same three sets of clothes since we got her," I told my friend Phillip on the phone. "I'm just too tired to go buy anything."

The next day, he brought over a huge bag of clothing in various sizes his daughter had outgrown. There were dozens of outfits and sleepers, and most of them fit. I almost cried. That sack of used clothing was one of the best gifts we could have received.

We took Adelynn to the pediatrician within her first few days home for a complete physical and to evaluate her vaccinations. According to her Chinese medical report she was perfectly healthy and current on her shots, but records are often inaccurate. There is some concern the vaccinations may not have been given to the children. Also, the vaccines, if administered, may have expired or been improperly stored, so the effectiveness was in question. Our pediatrician was educated on internationally adopted children and knew we needed to do extensive testing for a variety of illnesses. A child in an orphanage could be exposed to a variety of diseases and poisons. It was important to assess her completely. Jeff and two nurses had to hold Adelynn down while they drew over two tablespoons of blood from her tiny arm. I stood aside and bit my knuckles as Adelynn struggled and shrieked in pain. She was tested for Hepatitis A, B, and C, HIV, lead poisoning, nutritional deficiencies, and other disorders. The doctor looked at the open sores on the back of her head and the developing bumps on her hands and feet, and diagnosed scabies. Scabies is a contagious skin disease caused by mites that burrow under the skin and deposit their eggs.[17] Often people associate scabies with unclean living conditions. This isn't always true. Masses of children living in poor conditions are susceptible to them. It's very difficult to get rid of with so many children passing the mites back and forth, even if the caregivers were trying to do so. The doctor prescribed a cream for the scabies and medicine for Adelynn's lingering ear infection. The doctor noticed a Mongolian spot on her lower back. Mongolian spots are birthmarks common among people of Asian, East Indian, African, and Latino heritage.[18] They appear at birth, resembling a bruise. They are often located on the base of the spine, on the buttocks and back, but usually fade away by the teenage years. We hadn't even noticed the slight discoloration, but our pediatrician did. It was important to document the Mongolian spot so that the birthmark wouldn't be mistaken for a bruise. The visit and drawing of blood was traumatic enough without adding any immunizations, so we scheduled her series of vaccinations for the following week.

Since we had been skin-to-skin with Adelynn for almost two weeks, we were at risk of contracting scabies, too. We stripped and washed all the bedding and thoroughly vacuumed the entire house, even the areas of the carpet we usually neglect. Neither Jeff nor I had seen any signs of them on us, but it was a good precaution for us to be treated as well. We each had to completely cover ourselves, head to toe, with the scentless prescription cream.

"Do I really need to rub this stuff between my toes?" Jeff questioned my explicit instructions.

"If one of those buggies finds refuge between your toes because you didn't put cream there, we might have to go through this again. Start rubbing those piggies!" He rolled his eyes and squeezed another blob from the tube.

I certainly did not want to catch scabies and did exactly as the prescription directed. We slept covered in the cream, sticking to the sheets as we tossed in bed. We were able to wash it off the next morning. We never caught scabies, and Adelynn's sores eventually healed. Unfortunately, she still has the scars on the back of her head as a reminder.

◆   ◆   ◆

Getting Adelynn to sleep was a complicated ordeal. I would nestle her close in my arms and rock her while giving her a bottle. She enjoyed her bottle and would make eye contact with me while I sang to her. Adelynn liked a lot of rocking and singing. Before becoming a parent, I didn't have any reason to learn lullabies or children's songs. I discovered I was unprepared for bedtime songs. I would sing her song after song to help her relax, but eventually I ran out of songs to which I knew all the words.

"Oh, sit right back and you'll hear a tale, a tale of a fateful trip," I quietly sang, grateful to be able to pull another song from memory.

I grew up singing in our church choir where my dad played the organ and my mother sang soprano, so I did know some anthems. I knew every word of the "Hallelujah Chorus" but didn't know the third line to "I'm a Little Teapot." I developed my own repertoire of Christmas carols, church anthems, and TV sitcom theme songs. "I Am the Bread of the Life" was followed up with the theme song to "The Brady Bunch." I'd rock and sing until my throat became parched. Adelynn seemed to enjoy the variety and eventually would drift off to sleep.

Adelynn would sleep deeply the first hour then awaken in a sweaty fit of terror, shrieking and pulling fistfuls of hair. While we were still in China, we had witnessed her pulling her hair when she was nervous or scared. She had no hair on the back of her head where her sores were located. The itchiness of the scabies must have been unbearable. This hair pulling was something she did out of anxiety, habit, or maybe to self-soothe. No consoling seemed to help when she'd awaken in these rages. I'd pick her up and talk to her, so she'd know where she was, but she was half asleep and it didn't help.

"Momma loves you. I'm here," I'd say over and over again.

"You're safe with Momma and Daddy. It's okay. It's okay," I'd whisper.

She was like a wild animal. Her body would arch and twist, and she'd claw at her own skin. I didn't know what to do to help her.

These episodes are sometimes called night terrors. Even children who haven't suffered trauma can experience them. I'd rock and sing her back to sleep, but as soon as I tried to put her back in her crib her eyes bolted open and the screaming resumed. In desperation, I tried warming her crib sheet with a heating pad. Just before I'd lay her down, I'd pull the pad away and gently place her down on the warm bed. She'd awaken instantly, almost angrier upon discovering my unsuccessful trick. Anything to do with her crib was traumatic. She was terrified in it. I could only imagine that perhaps many nights in the orphanage she laid there screaming with no one responding to her cries. After two weeks of all night rocking, walking, singing and holding, we gave up forcing her to sleep in her crib and let her sleep in bed with us. She obviously needed us near, and it didn't feel natural to be all snuggly during the day but force her to sleep alone at night. She needed the security of our closeness, and we needed some sleep.

Adelynn's fears were just as intense as her confidence and drive. Some situations would send her into hysteria, while other times she'd amaze us with her courage. She was completely unafraid of animals, bugs or loud noises. She had great physical strength and effortlessly scaled furniture. She'd squeal with delight as Jeff tossed her high into the air and would swing her by her legs.

"Jeff, stop it," his mother would shriek, "you'll dislocate her legs!"

"More, more, Daddy," Adelynn would shout, not wanting the ride to end.

Friends and family would be startled at her fearlessness, but if we sat her in a chair she'd scream and sob. She was terrified of anything she had to sit on. We attribute the fear to the bamboo chairs she was locked in during the day at the orphanage. Her personality prefers predictability and security. If she felt out of control, she became very frightened.

The first fear we had to overcome was the car seat. This was one seat she absolutely had to adapt to. We brought the seat into the house and let her see it, crawl on it and put her little doll in it. Then we moved it to the car and let her play with it there. We would strap her in, wait a few minutes and unstrap her, so she'd get the idea the confinement wasn't permanent. Within a few days she would ride in her seat with someone sitting beside her. By the first week home, she was riding in her seat for short trips to the store. We were impressed with her progress and knew this assimilation method was how we needed to address her fears. We used a similar process to get her accustomed to the high chair and stroller. Within a few weeks she was sitting for meals and strolling through the mall.

Every day unveiled a new discovery in Adelynn's life. She grew to love the water. We had a small inflatable swimming pool given to us as a baby shower gift. I'd roll it into the front yard and fill it with clean water every sunny afternoon. In less than an hour, the hot summer sun would warm the water to bath water temperature, perfect for Adelynn to splash in. Walking on the grass, however, was not an option. The feel of the grass on her bare feet sent her into shaking horror. She didn't even like walking on it with sandals on. The grass could have been unfamiliar to her, or she may have simply not liked the feel of it on her feet. I'd carry her from the house to the pool, and she'd gratefully enter the water. If a blade of grass landed into the water she'd say "ah oh," and I would scoop it out. Once the grass was safely out of reach, she'd kick her tan legs in the water, and happily splash with her hands.

Adelynn was very alert and aware. The developmental delays we had anticipated never appeared. At less than fourteen months of age, and after only two months immersed in English, she could say words like "bottle," "light," "dada," "momma," "hot," "please," "bye-bye," "yeah," "tickle," "poo-poo," "okay," "baby," "right there," "push," and dozens more. She comprehended words quickly and understood simple instructions almost immediately. She was demonstrating an exceptional ability to grasp languages. This is not typical for international adoptees. Verbal and physical delays are common due to the lack of stimulation, nutrition and nurturing in an institutional setting. Adelynn's verbal and physical skills may have been an indication of her receiving a higher level of care at the orphanage, or she may simply be a bright and determined little girl. It was rewarding to watch her learn. Child development is a fascinating process.

I knew caring for a child would be difficult, but nothing can truly prepare someone for the day-to-day reality. I was adjusting to being a mother, as she was adjusting to her new world. I loved her very much and felt blessed to have her in our lives, but parenthood was still very demanding. It was challenging both physically and mentally. I had to be on continuous guard for anything that might poison, choke or cause injury. It seemed like everything was a potential threat. I worked to provide a stimulating environment for Adelynn and it didn't come naturally to me. I would watch other parents play with their children and try to pick up some tips. I didn't seem to know how to play with her. I had to learn that throwing a napkin on your head and letting it fall off is funny to a child. And whatever is funny must be done over and over again. We sang "The Wheels on the Bus" so many times I thought my brain would explode. Repetition can sometimes feel like work.

I found it awkward and shameful to discuss my inadequacies and frustrations with other mothers. When asked how we were adjusting, I learned most people really didn't want to know. Or if they did, they didn't want to hear anything but a happy report. What I was feeling was normal and not uncommon for any new parent. No one wants to be labeled a "bad mother," so I think many mothers don't discuss the negative feelings. I was lucky to have a few close friends who confided their secret fears and frustrations with me. It helped me to realize I was doing just fine, and things would become more natural with time.

Adelynn's desire to explore her surroundings increased. Even though she wasn't sleeping well, she showed no evidence of fatigue during the day. I had hoped my daughter would be a night owl and enjoy staying up late and sleeping in, but Adelynn was both a night owl and an early bird. She would fight bedtime, be awake on and off most of the night, and then ready for play at six a.m. Adelynn was able to walk from room to room while holding our hands and wanted to do so over and over from the moment she woke up. My body was suffering from lack of rest, and walking Adelynn around the house stooped over was torture on my back. The entire right side of my back was tingly and numb, and I often had shooting pains that would almost knock me to the ground. The daily activities of changing diapers, playing, and holding Adelynn were a struggle for me. I went to my doctor to see if I had damaged something in my back. The pain was very bad, and it became difficult to carry Adelynn and place her in and out of her car seat. My back was reacting to motherhood. I had missed the warm-up phase of adding pregnancy pounds to my body a little at a time. My back was feeling the shock of fatigued muscles from lack of sleep and the strain of carrying and lifting a child. The doctor prescribed an anti-inflammatory and pain reliever, but his non-verbal advice as a father of four was "get used to it."

It was important for Adelynn and I not to be "shut ins," so I made it a point to keep us active and with other people. We went to playgroups, story time, and lunches with friends. In hindsight, I realize I shouldn't have pushed myself to participate so quickly. Adelynn and I both needed time to adjust. I was tired and exhausted from her sleep disturbances. Her behavior was still unpredictable, but staying at home was monotonous. I remember quite vividly one particular playgroup we attended. A group of mothers and their children were spending an afternoon together playing and visiting. I was doing more listening than talking since I was so sleep deprived. One of the women tried to engage me in conversation and asked, "Isn't motherhood just magical?"

I'm sure my face must have gone white.

"Magical?" I thought, "Is that what I'm experiencing?" I was too tired to fake a response. "Uh, yeah" I said dryly, "Magical."

The look on her face showed pity, almost like she thought I was experiencing a depression or transition difficulty. I wasn't the one experiencing transition difficulty. Adelynn was. Or was she? The woman's cheeriness was annoying, and her pity irritated me. Were my sleep deprivation, numb back and shooting neck pains magical? Was it magical when Adelynn would suddenly burst into a fit of hysteria and I didn't know why? I must have been "feeling the magic" when what little free time I had was spent cleaning the house, washing dishes, doing laundry, paying bills, and preparing for the next repetitive day. The ladies told how their lives were now complete by having children, and they'd never experienced so much joy. I felt like I was the only one in the room who wasn't blissfully full of motherhood glee. Was there something wrong with me? I missed being able to sleep. I missed being able to wake up when I wanted and not when little fingers were prying open my eyes. I missed taking hot showers without the curtain being tugged and shampoo bottles tossed at my feet. I missed being able to relax and not think about how a cough drop wrapper could kill if choked on. Parenthood wasn't feeling magical.

Adelynn's sleeping problems became an escalating issue. She would awaken repetitively during the night and let out a shriek that seemed to come from deep inside her, literally forcing her body awake. It was a cry of fear, sadness, and intense anxiety. If I turned on the light and let her see where she was, she'd often settle back down. Sometimes holding her helped, sometimes it made it worse. She would wake up in cycles most of the night. She'd wake up every ten minutes, twenty minutes, or, if we were lucky, every forty minutes. It was as if as soon as she fell into a deep sleep something bolted her awake. She continued this pattern until about three in the morning, then she'd sleep somewhat soundly for an hour or two until the screaming would begin again. Jeff developed an incredible ability to sleep through it. He coped with the stress and fatigue by shutting down completely once he was asleep. I'm not sure how, but he would be fast asleep with her screaming hysterically, less than three inches from his ear. I think men and women must be wired differently. I, on the other hand, lay there, wide-awake, muscles tensed, anticipating the next wave of gasping cries.

The first few months home I attributed Adelynn's night screaming to an understandable adjustment period. Then her teething seemed like the culprit. When she had one of her "bad nights" I pondered that maybe she ate something that didn't agree with her, or she might be lactose intolerant. Could she have the flu, or was she disturbed because of the busy day we had? After six months of sleep problems, I knew we needed to do something. If I slept a combined total of three hours during the night I felt lucky. Never in my life have I ever experienced that degree of sleep deprivation. My entire body hurt as I went about my day in a daze.

I was sorting shapes with Adelynn on the floor one afternoon when, in what seemed like a blink, she was gone. I had fallen asleep sitting up, and she was in another room. I was doing crazy things. I found the mail in the refrigerator and milk under the sink. While driving the car, I fell asleep at the stoplights. I became dangerously fatigued. I would joke if there was ever a "Sleepless Survivor" show, I'd walk away the winner. It was truly amazing to me that I continued to function as long as I did with only fragments of sleep. Something had to change.

I kept a sleep journal of when Adelynn got up in the morning, took her nap, went to bed, and how many times she woke in the night. Once I put down on paper what was happening I became alarmed.

"Jeff, she's waking up screaming almost thirty times a night!" I was concerned there might be a medical problem, so I did some research on the Internet for answers. Some possible causes of these dramatic sleep problems could be, of course, emotional, such as post-traumatic stress disorder or reactive attachment disorder. We consulted an ear, nose and throat specialist to rule out sleep apnea, enlarged tonsils or adenoids. The doctor examined her but found nothing contributing to her sleep disturbances. Oddly, I was disappointed when the doctor said she was perfectly normal. If there was something physically wrong with her that caused the sleep problems, at least we could fix it. Emotional problems were far more complicated. I was frustrated, saddened, and worn out.

We visited with our pediatric psychologist, who was well experienced with adoptive children, to discuss possible emotional problems causing her sleep disturbances. He was concerned the rhythmic nature of her screams could be related to nighttime seizures. It was unlikely, but something that needed to be ruled out. She had an electroencephalogram (EEG) to test her brain waves for any unusual activity. In the EEG, over twenty electrodes were glued on her scalp to detect and record the electrical impulses within the brain. It was required that she have at least four hours less sleep than usual. Apparently most children fall asleep during the procedure. Not Adelynn. She didn't like the glue or wires, and was unhappy about the entire process. She screamed and struggled for an entire hour. Fortunately, everything was normal, but I felt bad that we had put her through the test unnecessarily. At the time, we didn't want to miss any medical causes for her sleep disturbances and needed to rule out every possibility.

Once all medical causes were eliminated, we were left with the realization that Adelynn was experiencing emotional distress at night from a past trauma. It was possible she was suffering from a form of post-traumatic stress disorder. Her trauma could have been abuse, neglect, transition, or other unknown causes. In addition to counseling, our pediatrician and pediatric psychologist suggested we give her something to help her sleep through the night. The lack of sleep was unhealthy for her, and it needed to change. The goal of a sleeping drug was to assist her in settling down and teach her to change her sleeping habits. I wish I could say I fought the idea and proclaimed to the doctors I would never put my baby on a drug. The reality was, however, I was excited about the idea of sleeping again and eagerly accepted the medicine. Much to my amazement, the medicine provided a great improvement. It didn't knock her out cold, only calmed her down. She still tossed and turned a lot, but gone were the nights of endless screaming. The medicine was just enough to take the edge off. The screaming was replaced with sighs and talking which was much easier to withstand in the middle of the night. I'd awaken to her saying, "Grandpa, hair, all gone" (her Grandpa is bald) instead of her scratching at her face, screaming with fear, and thrashing around. It was a welcome change. We kept her on the medicine for a little over three weeks and then decided to try backing her off of it. Apparently, those three weeks were all she needed to reprogram for better sleeping. She still has night disturbances a few times a week, they haven't totally gone away, but it's a vast improvement from thirty times a night. I often wonder what would have happened if we had given her the medicine sooner. It might have saved us a few months of sleepless nights, but I think some of her anxieties needed to be released. Raising a child is an on-going experiment of what to do and what not to do. We make an educated guess and hope for the best.

◆   ◆   ◆

Once our sleep schedule straightened out, everything else in our lives got better. A little sleep can heal a world of problems. Adelynn was easier to handle during the day and my patience was better. I had more energy to do fun things with her, instead of just focusing on surviving the day. Our favorite game we play is imagination. Adelynn loves playing pretend with her elaborate kitchen set given to her by Grandma and Grandpa at Christmas.

"Momma, hot tea," Adelynn says as she hands me a tiny plastic cup. "Good, Momma?"

I pretend to sip my drink. "Mmm, delicious!"

She hands me a plate with assorted wooden shapes. "Time to eat, Momma."

"Ooo, what's for dinner?" I'm always curious what she'll come out with.

"Pizza, ca-cumbers, and nips," she announces with pride. What a wonderful hostess!

We both enjoy singing and I have since learned the words to more children's songs than I care to repeat. The songs haunt me in my sleep and throughout the day.

"How I love my flubber, blubber, flubber, blubber, flubber, blubber, how I love my flubber, blubber, whale, blubber, whale, how I love my flubber, blubber whale." Who writes these songs?

It took me some time, but I finally learned to ask for more help from Jeff and my mom. I arranged for Adelynn to visit my mom every Thursday morning. This would become our routine, and I was guaranteed at least one morning a week to do whatever I wanted to recharge. My personal time is vital to me being the best mom I can be. Making time to spend with friends, like Dana and Charlene, revitalizes me and reassures me I'm doing okay. There's nothing more therapeutic than the encouragement of a friend who has experienced the same challenges and has overcome them.

Jeff needs his time too, so we've arranged a schedule for him to have a few hours each week to enjoy his hobbies. He likes woodworking, home remodeling and riding his bike. He has since lost the twenty pounds he gained during our first six months of sleep exhaustion.

Adelynn is blessed with a supportive family. She has grown very close to her grandparents. Jeff takes Adelynn to his mother's house every Sunday. It's valuable time with his side of the family and gives me a few hours to myself. On Sunday morning, Adelynn automatically knows she's going to memaw's.

"Memaw's house, eat mah-fins?" she asks springing out of bed at a very early hour. Her memaw has a tradition of making fresh muffins for their visit. With a sticky muffin in her hand, Adelynn and her memaw laugh and chase each other around the house.

My mom is retired and able to see Adelynn almost every other day. Adelynn is either going for a visit or Mom is meeting us at one of Adelynn's activities. She is my mom's only grandchild and one of the best things that has ever happened in her life. Her spirit is renewed and she's overflowing with love for Adelynn.

My dad, her papa, loves sneaking up on her and whisking her into the air.

"Papa, git you," she says with excited wide eyes and almost exploding with squeals. She dramatically runs away from him but just close enough for him to grab her.

"Grraah, got ya," Papa will shout as he lifts her high into the air.

"No, Papa, no," she shouts while giggling and pretending to put up a fight.

My parents are very easy-going grandparents. Once thrifty and reserved, anything for Adelynn is happily accepted. Once, eating out in a restaurant, my dad was playing the "Gotcha!" game with Adelynn, and in a dramatic lunge of his arm he knocked his meal off the table. He and Adelynn laughed together.

"Who are you people?" I asked my carefree parents as they picked the mess up off the floor. Playing at the table would not have been tolerated when I was growing up.

"Being a grandparent is all the fun of being a parent without the stress and responsibility," my mother explained as my dad playfully flipped a piece of fruit at Adelynn.

I didn't grow up near my grandparents and realize now what I missed. The relationship between grandparent and grandchild is a precious thing.

Closing Thoughts from a New Mother

o o o o o o o o o o o o o o o o o o o o o o o o o o o o o o o o

Words are the voice of the heart.

——*Confucius*

Our entire adoption process took twenty-one months to complete. In the midst of the paperwork gathering, interviews, and waiting, the process felt complicated, intrusive, and painful. It was our "labor" required to "deliver" our daughter home. Much like labor, with time you forget the pain. Adelynn is worth every bit of it. My only regret is that the process didn't move faster. What a long year it must have been for Adelynn to endure in the orphanage. While she waited for parents, we waited for our daughter.

Adelynn's initial adjustment was neither typical nor atypical. All children handle the transition in different ways. I've heard of children who adapted easily into their new homes, and for others the change was devastating. Adelynn's sleep problems were greater than most families have to face, but as in everything in life, we have our blessings and challenges.

Looking at her referral pictures today makes me cry. I know my daughter very well. I look at the pictures of her back then and know exactly what she's feeling. The look in her dark eyes is of fear, sadness, and longing. I can see the waiting look in her eyes. It pains me to think it took so long for us to get to her. As I pull out the precious memories and details of Adelynn's life from our storage box, I'm overwhelmed with emotion. I'm particularly moved holding the shoes she was wearing when she was handed to us. The tiny plastic sandals, worn and tattered, are a grim reminder of her life at the orphanage.

It's important for us to keep Adelynn's Chinese heritage alive. Before we brought her home we anticipated including Chinese cultural activities in our lives and being involved in the Chinese community. What we have found is, we forget she's Chinese. She's Adelynn, our daughter. We don't see race. It's something we'll have to work on. Teaching her about China, exposing her to the language, visiting the country and attending events that cater to internationally adopted children will become part of our life. She's a Chinese-American, and both aspects of her identity are important. Out in public people will make comments reminding me she's Chinese. Strangers see an adopted Chinese girl. I'm still adjusting to the amount of attention we receive. People love children. They seem to be drawn to them, and a Chinese girl with a red headed six-foot tall mother draws attention. Wherever we go, we get noticed. I've become an ambassador of Chinese adoptions, whether I want to be or not. Most people are interested in why she doesn't look like me, where she's from, and how she got here. They sometimes toss out an uneducated comment like, "They throw away their baby girls over there, don't they?" They aren't thinking the baby girl is standing in front of them, listening to every word.

Adelynn couldn't be any more our daughter than if we had conceived her. Her personality and sense of humor fit our family perfectly. Watching her sleep, I feel an intense love that makes me feel complete and secure, yet also frightens me to my core. I absolutely cannot let myself think about something devastating happening to her. It's too terrifying to even consider. I've never given birth to a child, so I can't speak on the birth child/adoptive child comparison, but I can honestly say it would not have made any difference in how we feel about her. Adelynn's our little miracle and we're so blessed to have her in our lives.

I'm touched to see how gentle and kind she is to our dogs. She loves them and enjoys assisting with their care. She helps spoon the moist dog food into their bowls and stirs in the kibbles to just the right consistency.

During their bath, she offers them doggy cookies so they won't be scared and talks them through the experience. She reminds me to give Marcie her daily allergy medication and says, "May-a-sin for skin. Good girl, Marcie," when Marcie swallows her pills. Andrew gained ten pounds the first six months Adelynn was home. His pleading eyes were successful in receiving extra treats from the high chair. I still catch Adelynn sneaking food to him under the table. He's expanding to enormous proportions!

Finding a balance and managing my new life has become a huge challenge. There are dozens of things in my day that require and compete for my attention. I strive to be a loving, devoted mother and spend meaningful time with my daughter. Keeping a journal of Adelynn's childhood, building photo albums, and scrap-booking memories are important. I love my husband and want to nurture our marriage with time together, just the two of us. I have extended family and friends who require my time and attention and three dogs needing baths, shots, food, and affection. Time to myself is important to enjoy my hobbies, volunteer work, and my voice-over business. Our house is a bottomless pit of need, requiring cleaning, laundry, cooking, shopping, and repair. My body demands a healthy lifestyle with regular exercise, a good night's sleep and proper diet. Each of these things is important, but every day something gets neglected. I'm accustomed to achieving my personal goals and feel inadequate that I can't do it all. I prioritize and do my best but fall short every day. I do a little when I can, but never get caught up. I see other mothers who are "super mom" types and wonder how they do it. How do they manage their time to be able to do everything? What are they neglecting? Themselves, maybe? I'm still learning this tricky balancing act.

Thankfully, Adelynn LOVES to travel! We worried that our travel days were over, but that hasn't been the case. She's already made a few domestic trips and celebrated her second birthday crossing the Atlantic, returning from a week in Paris. She seems to come by it naturally.

"Momma, right there, airplane!" she yells with excitement from the back seat of the car.

"I see it," I confirm and return her wide-eyed expression.

"Vacation with Mickey, BIG boat in water," my adorable two year old recites, recalling her Disney Cruise taken months prior.

We've been known to picnic in a grassy field across from the airport. We nibble sandwiches while watching the planes take off and land. We pretend the passengers have just returned from exotic trips abroad. According to Adelynn, most of the visitors travel to visit Mickey Mouse.

Our love for Adelynn continues to blossom more each day. She has added a depth to our marriage I never knew was possible. Although I still miss some of the simpler aspects of my life before becoming a parent, I'm amazed at the amount of fulfillment she's added. Watching her learn a new task or overcome a fear, gives me great satisfaction even though it's truly her accomplishment. Precious moments together bring me peace and contentment.

"Momma, twinkle, twinkle, please," she requests while climbing on our bed. I have a pounding headache but never pass up the opportunity to snuggle. Lying on the bed together, nose-to-nose, I feel her warm breath on my face as she sings the classic song.

"Twinkle, twinkle lee-tal star," she sings while opening and closing her delicate hands as if they were twinkling stars. We've sung this hundreds of times together, but I never tire of it. Watching her little lips purse to form the words brings happiness to my soul.

"Like a die-mund een thuh skah." She sings the word "sky" sounding like a true Oklahoman. I listen as she finishes the song flatly but with passion.

When the song is over she twirls my hair around her fingers and asks, "Momma?"

"Yes, Adelynn," I respond, touched by her loving gesture.

"Momma's head hurt?" she asks while caressing my forehead. "My-gain?"

"Yes, honey, Momma has a migraine." She leans over and grabs the ice pack I'm holding on my head.

"Ay-ya hold for Momma," she whispers while holding the cold pack against my temple. "Momma, okay?" she asks tilting her head with empathy.

"Momma will be okay," I reassure her. "I just need some rest."

Adelynn takes my hand in hers, leans over and kisses me on the lips. "Oh, my momma hurt," she says quietly while shaking her head like a worried mother. "Momma rest your body," she instructs while patting my hand. "Ay-ya loves you."

Her compassion takes my breath away. "I love you, too, Adelynn," I whisper, humbled to be her mother. It just doesn't get much better than this. Yes, being a mother IS magical!

Family Photographs

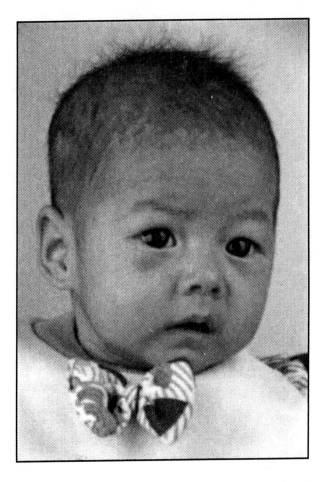

The referral picture of Ji Chen Ge, soon to be Adelynn Chen-Ge
Woodard.

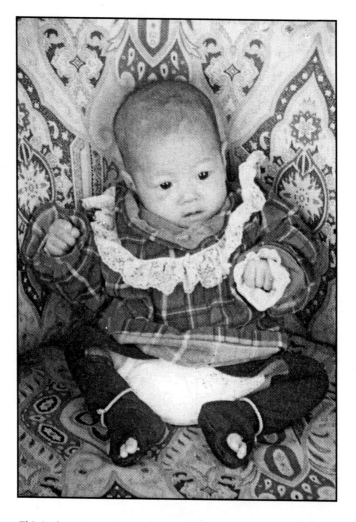

This is the referral picture that brings me to tears. Her eyes speak volumes!

*This picture was taken only seconds after they placed Adelynn in my
arms for the very first time.*

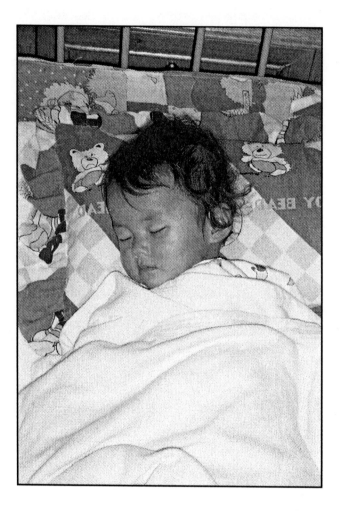

Adelynn's first night with us, sleeping in the hotel crib.

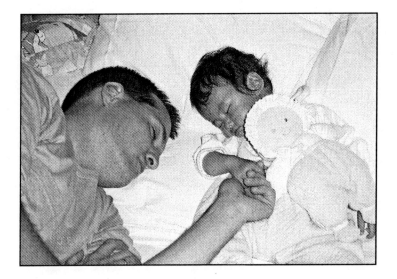

Another sleeping picture, but too precious to leave out. Adelynn's second night, fast asleep with her daddy.

Adelynn giving Andrew a big hug. She had only been home two days when this picture was taken. No fear of dogs!

Daddy and Adelynn spending a Saturday afternoon at the pool.

Adelynn's most famous trick, mid-air splits! Picture taken at seventeen months old.

In our garden wearing her favorite character, Winnie the Pooh.

Adelynn and Momma, two lives changed forever!

Personal Questions about Adopting from China

I'm including some personal questions many people have about adopting from China, but are too polite to ask. Actually, many people have asked me these questions, but it's considered rather rude to do so.

1. How much did she "cost?"

I'd like to clarify that babies aren't "bought" from China. There are many expenses required to fund an adoption. There is a donation made to the orphanage and some legal expenses, but most of the expenses are for paperwork and traveling. Our total adoption costs were just under $20,000. This included paperwork processing, international travel expenses, agency fees, and fees in China. There is currently a $10,000 tax credit in place for adoption expenses. The tax credit is an actual credit, not a deduction. After the adoption is finalized, qualifying families can receive a $10,000 refund. This was not in effect at the time our adoption was finalized, but it is a huge help for families today.

2. Do you think you'll have children of "your own?"

No, if we have more children, and that's a big if, we would certainly adopt again. We are thrilled with our daughter and would adopt another child from China if we wanted more children. The correct term is "birth child," not "your own" or "real daughter." To say Adelynn isn't "our own" or our "real daughter" insinuates she isn't our daughter. It's more than a politically correct thing. It makes a difference to the child who hears it. I dread the day someone asks us right in front of her, "Will you ever have children of your own?"

3. Don't you ever wonder about her "real" parents?

She's not our faux or fake daughter, she's real! And we're her real parents, the people who have raised her, cared for her, survived her sleep distur-bances and illnesses. Regarding her birth parents, I don't think about where she came from, who she looks like, or where her birth family is. I think it's because I just see her as our daughter. All of these issues are important parts of her, but on a day-to-day basis I forget she's adopted from China. Just last week I was at a playgroup with a group of moms. They were comparing the height of their children to their own height. I jumped right in the middle of the conversation saying, "Adelynn is tall and lean just like me. I hope she has Jeff's coordination." It flew out of my mouth without thinking. I truly forget she didn't come from my gene pool.

4. She doesn't look Chinese. Could she be mixed with another race?

As Americans, we have a picture in our minds of what a typical Chinese person looks like. Short, lean body, black straight hair, and Asian eyes. Everyone in Ireland doesn't have red hair, and all Italians don't have big noses. It's a stereotype. Adelynn is tall, with wavy hair, and almond eyes. She's still Chinese.

5. Are you going to tell her she's adopted?

This question makes me laugh. Wouldn't she eventually figure this out? Yes, we began talking to Adelynn about her story from the very beginning. I used the first few months home as practice for wording the explanation. Now at two years old, she recognizes the mention of China, understands she flew on an airplane, and has seen pictures of Jeff and me before we had a daughter. She understands that we flew to China to bring her home. That's a good start. We'll continue age-appropriate discussions about her Chinese culture, heritage and adoption. I anticipate she'll read this book in her teens.

Notes

1   Karin Evans, *The Lost Daughters of China, Abandoned Girls, Their Journey to America, and the Search for a Missing Past* (New York: Jeremy P. Tarcher/Putnam, 2000).

2   Population and Development Review, Vol. 24 No. 3, September 1998.

3   "Desire for Sons Drives Use of Prenatal Scans in China," *New York Times,* by Erik Eckholm, June 21, 2002.

4   "China Thrown Off Balance as Boys Outnumber Girls," *USA TODAY*, Paul Wiseman, June 19, 2002.

5   "China Improves Care of Abandoned Children," *Cnews*, by Martin Fackler, February 3, 2001.

6   "International Adoption Facts," *The Evan B. Donaldson Adoption Institute*, 2002, Adoptioninstitute.org.

7   Quotation from *Post-Traumatic Stress Disorder in Post-Institutionalized Children* by Laura Beck, Nancy D'Antonio, and Lynne Lyon from AttachChina.com with the kind permission of author Nancy D'Antonio.

8   Dillon International, 3227 East 31st Street, Suite 200, Tulsa, Oklahoma 74105 Tel: 918.749.4600.

9   Families with Children from China is an organization of families who have adopted children from China. FCC's purpose is to provide a support network for families who've adopted from China and for prospective parents. **www.fwcc.org**.

10   Attach-China is a website dedicated to educating parents of children adopted from China about Reactive Attachment Disorder. **http://members.aol.com/RADchina/index.html**.

11   Brian Kilcommons, Sarah Wilson, *Childproofing Your Dog, A Complete Guide to Preparing Your Dog for the Children in Your Life* (Warner Books: Incorporated, 1994).

12   For a picture of the figurine visit: **http://www.dollsales.com/Bears/ momma%20&%20poppa%20with%20mcnewbear.htm**.

13   Helpful packing lists located at: **http://www.fwcc.org/packtips.htm**.

14   Lotus Travel is a travel agency that creates adoptive family travel packages. Their popular "Ladybug Package" allows adoptive families to fly business class at a fraction of the cost. Tel: 800 956 8873 **www.lotustours.net** Email: **info@lotustours.net**.

15   Linda Acredolo, Ph. D., and Susan Goodwyn, Ph. D., *Baby Signs, How to Talk with Your Baby Before Your Baby Can Talk* (Illinois: Contemporary Books, 1992).

16   Danny's Bagel is a delivery service in Guangzhou, China, specializing in Italian/American food. **www.dannysbagel.com**.

17   "Scabies," *YAHOO! Health*, 2002, http://health.yahoo.com/.

18   "An Insider's Guide to Transracial Adoption," *PACT, An Adoption Alliance*, by Gail Steinberg and Beth Hall, **http://www.pactadopt.org**.

Helpful Resources

Dillon International
Dillon has been placing internationally born infants and children with U.S. families in all 50 states and overseas since 1972.
3227 East 31st Street, Suite 200
Tulsa, Oklahoma 74105
Tel: 918 749 4600
www.dillonadopt.com
Email: info@dillonadopt.com

Families with Children from China
Families with Children from China (FCC) is an organization of families who have adopted children from China. FCC's purpose is to provide a support network for families who've adopted from China and for prospective parents. There are links on this website to anything you ever wanted to know about adopting from China.
www.fwcc.org

Adoptive Parents of China
Adoptive Parents of China is an email group for persons who are interested in the process or have adopted children from the People's Republic of China. This is a very active list, and I relied on it extensively as a source of information and support during our process.
http://groups.yahoo.com/group/a-parents-china/

Rainbow Kids
Rainbow Kids is a free online international adoption publication. This website is a great place to start if you're considering adoption from any country.
www.rainbowkids.com

The Red Thread Magazine
The Red Thread Magazine is a website and magazine focused on the interests of adoptive families and families waiting for Chinese children.
www.redthreadmag.com

Asia For Kids
Asia for Kids is a resource for language and cultural items.
www.asiaforkids.com

Celebrate the Child
Celebrate the Child is an on-line store with cultural and adoptive items.
www.celebratechild.com

China Sprout
China Sprout is a website providing Chinese cultural products and services.
www.chinasprout.com

Sarah Lynn Woodard
Please visit my website for a current list of helpful resources. You may also contact me for any comments or questions through this site.
www.DaughterFromAfar.com

The Book's Fundraiser

$1 from each book sold will be donated to the "Home of Joy" project, supported by Dillon International. "Home of Joy" is an orphanage located in northern China. Donations will be used to provide food, clothing, vitamins, and medicines as well as to provide much needed corrective surgeries for some of the children in the orphanage.

Thank you very much for purchasing this book and contributing to the "Home of Joy" project. Additional donations may be sent to:

Development Director
Dillon International
3227 East 31st Street, Suite 200
Tulsa, Oklahoma 74105

0-595-24543-9

Printed in the United States
1514900005B/151-153